BTM

REAL ENGLISH

SPEAKING

1

Beginning

Audios on Youtube: #BtmRealEnglish

All inquiries should be addressed to:

Book Domain LLC.
543 E Louise Dr Phoenix, Az 85050

Ordering Information:
Amount Deals. Special rebates are accessible on the amount bought by corporations, associations, and others. For points of interest, contact the distributor at the address above.

Printed in the United States of America.

ISBN-13   Paperback   978-1-964100-50-0
           eBook   978-1-964100-51-7

Library of Congress Control Number: 2025905689

BTM

REAL ENGLISH

SPEAKING

1

Beginning

<small>EDITED BY</small>

CHEOL BEOM LEE

BOOK DOMAIN LLC
Publish to Perfection

CONTENTS

UNIT 1

SKIT 1

GREETING AND TELLING NAME, ADDRESS, AGE, AND PHONE NUMBERS

2	Ms. Thomson:	Hi, everyone, welcome to BTM English class. My name is Sue Thompson.
3	Ms. Thomson:	I am your English teacher, and I'm so happy to see you all!
4	Jennifer:	Hi, Ms. Thompson.
5	Ms. Thomson:	Hi, what's your name?
6	Jennifer:	My name is Jennifer.
7	Ms. Thomson:	Hi Jennifer. Nice to meet you.
8	Jennifer:	Nice to meet you, too.
9	Ms. Thomson:	What's your last name?
10	Jennifer:	My last name is Park.
11	Ms. Thomson:	Where are you from, Jennifer?
12	Jennifer:	I am from New York, but my parents are from Korea.
13	Ms. Thomson:	Really? When did you move to Colorado?

14	Jennifer:	When I was five.
15	Ms. Thomson:	What's your father's name?
16	Jennifer:	Steve.
17	Ms. Thomson:	What's your mother's name?
18	Jennifer:	Diana.
19	Ms. Thomson:	That's a pretty name. One of my best friend is Diana as well!
20	Jennifer:	My mom loves her name. What a coincidence!
21	Ms. Thomson:	Where do you live?
22	Jennifer:	I live in North Boulder.
23	Ms. Thomson:	I see.
24	Jack:	I live in North Boulder too.
25	Ms. Thomson:	Is that right? What's your name?
26	Jack:	I'm Jack Smith.
27	Ms. Thomson:	What grade are you in, Jack?
28	Jack:	Second grade.
29	Ms. Thomson:	Where do you go to school?
30	Jack:	I go to Boulder Valley Elementary school.
31	Ms. Thomson:	Oh very cool! What is your favorite subject, Jack?
32	Jack:	I like gym class because it's very fun.
33	Ms. Thomson:	How do you like your school?
34	Jack:	I like it! The teachers are all very kind.
35	Ms. Thomson:	That's good. Do you have any siblings, Jack?
36	Jack:	Yes, I have a brother.
37	Ms. Thomson:	How old is he?
38	Jack:	He is five.
39	Ms. Thomson:	How old are you, Jack?

40	Jack:	I am eight years old.
41	Ms. Thomson:	How do you like your brother?
42	Jack:	He can be mean, but I like him.
43	Ms. Thomson:	What a good brother!
44	Jack:	Thank you.
45	Ms. Thomson:	Very nice, Jack. Do you have many friends?
46	Jack:	Yes, I do.
47	Ms. Thomson:	That's great! Many of your friends are here, right?
48	Jack:	Yes, they are.
49	Ms. Thomson:	What do you do with your friends, Jack?
50	Jack:	We just hang out a lot. Our parents set up play dates and let us have sleepovers!
51	Jane:	I love having sleepovers!
52	Ms. Thomson:	Oh I bet! They do sound like a lot of fun! What's your name?
53	Jane:	My name is Jane, and my last name is Kemper.
54	Ms. Thomson:	Very good, Jane! What do you like to do with your friends?
55	Jane:	We play on the playground, bike together after school, and sometimes have parties.
56	Ms. Thomson:	Wow, that sounds like a lot of fun! When do you have parties with your friends?
57	Jane:	When it's someone's birthday or to celebrate certain holidays.
58	Ms. Thomson:	Very nice. When is your birthday, Jane?
59	Jane:	May fifteenth.

60	Ms. Thomson:	What year?
61	Jane:	Two thousand four.
62	Ms. Thomson:	How do you invite your friends to your birthday party, Jane?
63	Jane:	I send them invitation cards.
64	Ms. Thomson:	Do you also make phone calls?
65	Jane:	Yes, I call them to make sure they are attending.
66	Ms. Thomson:	Do you have a phone, Jane?
67	Jane:	Yes, I do.
68	Ms. Thomson:	What's your phone number?
69	Jane:	Three oh three, nine nine seven, two four five six.
70	Ms. Thomson:	What do you put on your invitation?
71	Jane:	I put the time, date, and location of the party.
72	Ms. Thomson:	Do you play everyday with your friends?
73	Jane:	Yes, almost everyday.
74	Ms. Thomson:	Do they all live nearby?
75	Jane:	A lot of them do.
76	Ms. Thomson:	Oh that is very nice!
77	Joe:	Ms. Thompson?
78	Ms. Thomson:	Yes?
79	Joe:	Can I go to the bathroom?
80	Ms. Thomson:	Of course, you can. Do you know where it is?
81	Joe:	Yes, I do.
82	Ms. Thomson:	Okay! Hey, before you go, do you mind telling us your name?
83	Joe:	My name's Joe.
84	Ms. Thomson:	Alright Joe, you may be excused.

85	Tiffany:	Ms. Thompson, may I ask you a question?
86	Ms. Thomson:	Of course! What is your name by the way?
87	Tiffany:	Tiffany.
88	Ms. Thomson:	Hi, Tiffany. What's your question?
89	Tiffany:	Do we get a lot of homework for this class?
90	Ms. Thomson:	No, not really. I'm sure that you will enjoy doing any homework I give out for this class!
91	Tiffany:	Like what?
92	Ms. Thomson:	Like talking to your parents, and playing with your friends speaking English.
93	Tiffany:	Do we have homework for tomorrow?
94	Ms. Thomson:	(Joe comes back) Are you okay, Joe?
95	Joe:	Yes, I am fine. Thank you, Ms. Thompson.
96	Ms. Thomson:	No problem. Now, back to Tiffany's question. Yes, you will.
97	Tiffany:	What's the homework for tomorrow?
98	Ms. Thomson:	I want you to talk to your parents about fruits, vegetables, and your favorite things to do, all in English.
99	Tiffany:	That's easy.
100	Ms. Thomson:	Yes, it sure is! I told you homework will be fun and easy!
101	Tiffany:	Yes, you did. Thank you.
102	Ms. Thomson:	You are very welcome. We will stop here for today, and see you tomorrow. Bye everyone.

SKIT 2

TALKING ABOUT FRUITS AND VEGETABLES

2	Ms. Thomson:	Good afternoon everyone! How is everyone doing today?
3	Class:	Fine, thank you.
4	Ms. Thomson:	Good. Did everyone do their homework?
5	Class:	Yes.
6	Ms. Thomson:	Excellent. For review purposes, let's talk about edible fruits now.
7	Tiffany:	May I start first?
8	Ms. Thomson:	Of course you may. Can you list five fruits we can eat?
9	Tiffany:	I talked to my parents about a lot of fruits we can eat.
10	Ms. Thomson:	Very good. Can you tell us five kinds of fruit we can eat?
11	Tiffany:	Yes. Tomatoes, watermelons, oranges, bananas, and plums.
12	Ms. Thomson:	Excellent! Who can add five more to the list?

13	Joe:	I can. We talked about apples, pears, blueberries, peaches, and strawberries.
14	Ms. Thomson:	Great! Which one of those is your favorite, Joe?
15	Joe:	I like pears the most. They are so sweet and juicy.
16	Ms. Thomson:	Excellent. What other kinds of fruits are there that we can eat?
17	Jane:	What about persimmons, pineapples, mulberries, grapes, and cantaloupes?
18	Ms. Thomson:	Yes. You can eat all of those indeed! Let's have one more person list five fruits you can eat. Jack, how about you?
19	Jack:	What about dates, lemons, kiwis, raspberries, and mangos?
20	Ms. Thomson:	Great job. Wow, all these fruits are making my mouth water! Moving on, let's talk about vegetables. Who can list some vegetables for me?
21	Jennifer:	I can try! Should I just list five vegetables?
22	Ms. Thomson:	Yes, please.
23	Jennifer:	Onions, cabbage, carrots, eggplant, and cucumbers.
24	Ms. Thomson:	Great job. Who else can list a few vegetables for me?
25	Joe:	How about lettuce, iceberg lettuce, celery, potatoes, and kale?
26	Ms. Thomson:	Yes, they are all vegetables! Great job, Joe. Who else?

27	Jane:	Oh me! What about sweet potatoes, radishes, green onions, zucchini, and cilantro?
28	Ms. Thomson:	Good job, Jane. Are there any vegetables we missed?
29	Jane:	How about squash?
30	Ms. Thomson:	Good job, Jane.
31	Jane:	Thank you.
32	Ms. Thomson:	Wonderful. I think we've got enough vegetables. Now, let's talk about the things you like to do.
33	Note:	(Jack raises his hand)
34	Ms. Thomson:	Yes, Jack, go ahead.
35	Jack:	I like to play soccer with my dad.
36	Ms. Thomson:	Wonderful. How often do you play soccer with your dad, Jack?
37	Jack:	Every Saturday morning.
38	Ms. Thomson:	Where do you play soccer?
39	Jack:	At the park in our neighborhood.
40	Ms. Thomson:	Are you good at soccer?
41	Jack:	I think so. I like playing it very much!
42	Ms. Thomson:	Is there anything you don't like to do, Jack?
43	Jack:	Well, I don't like doing schoolwork.
44	Ms. Thomson:	I'm sure you're not the only one! I actually don't know many people who like to study. What makes you dislike studying?
45	Jack:	It's too boring.
46	Ms. Thomson:	Since you seem like a very active person, I understand that it can be a bit boring!
47	Jack:	Yeah, that's probably why.

48	Ms. Thomson:	Totally understandable!
49	Tiffany:	I don't like to study either! I do enjoy reading books, though.
50	Ms. Thomson:	Oh how strange! Studying and reading are interchangeable words, more often than not!
51	Tiffany:	Studying is hard, but reading is not.
52	Ms. Thomson:	Oh, I see what you mean now. If you can just enjoy reading things for school like you do while reading what you want, studying will become a lot easier!
53	Tiffany:	That's what my mother always says.
54	Ms. Thomson:	I am not surprised! You should definitely listen to her because she is absolutely right! Try to enjoy what you read for school more!
55	Tiffany:	I will try. Thank you.
56	Ms. Thomson:	You are welcome. Joe, what do you like to do?
57	Joe:	I like to watch sports games.
58	Ms. Thomson:	What sports do you like to watch, Joe?
59	Joe:	I like baseball and basketball.
60	Ms. Thomson:	Do you watch the games at home or at the stadium?
61	Joe:	I watch them at home on TV.
62	Ms. Thomson:	Do your parents watch the games with you as well?
63	Joe:	My father does. He really loves sports.
64	Ms. Thomson:	What does your mom like to do?
65	Joe:	I think my mom loves shopping.
66	Ms. Thomson:	What makes you think so, Joe?
67	Joe:	She is always out buying things.

68	Ms. Thomson:	I see. What about you, Jane?
69	Jane:	I like to visit my grandmother's place.
70	Ms. Thomson:	Wow, what does your grandmother do for you?
71	Jane:	She loves me very much. She always buys me many presents when I go to visit!
72	Ms. Thomson:	How often do you visit your grand-mother, Jane?
73	Jane:	About once a month.
74	Ms. Thomson:	Does she live nearby?
75	Jane:	Yes, she lives about an hour away.
76	Ms. Thomson:	How old is your grandmother?
77	Jane:	I don't know.
78	Ms. Thomson:	Does she live alone?
79	Jane:	Yes, she does. My grandfather passed away three years ago.
80	Ms. Thomson:	I am sorry to hear that.
81	Jane:	It's alright. My grandmother still talks a lot about him.
82	Ms. Thomson:	Oh I bet! Alright, I think that is enough for today. Tomorrow, we shall discuss things about our family members!
83	Jane:	Is that homework for tomorrow?
84	Ms. Thomson:	Yes, please come in ready to talk about your family members! Be ready to share their names, nicknames, birthdays, jobs, and anything else that is unique about them!
85	Jane:	Can I also talk about my relatives?
86	Ms. Thomson:	Of course. Feel free to talk about any-one of your family members. Okay, that will be it for today! See you tomorrow.

SKIT 3

TALKING ABOUT WEATHER
AND FAMILY

2	Ms. Thomson:	Good morning everyone!
3	Class:	Good morning, Ms. Thompson!
4	Ms. Thomson:	Wow, it's raining. Does anyone here like rainy days?
5	Jack:	No, I don't.
6	Ms. Thomson:	What's wrong with rainy days?
7	Jack:	I don't like to carry an umbrella when it rains.
8	Jennifer:	I do! I like to carry an umbrella. It's fun.
9	Tiffany:	Me too, I like when it rains cats and dogs.
10	Joe:	I don't mind rain, but I wish there were such things as rain days. You know, kind of like a snow day except with rain!
11	Ms. Thomson:	Who knows, we may end up having a rain day if it doesn't stop raining!
12	Tiffany:	May I ask you a question?
13	Ms. Thomson:	Sure, Tiffany.
14	Tiffany:	What's a rain check?

15	Ms. Thomson:	Good question, Tiffany. Has anyone heard of a 'rain check'?
16	Jack:	I have.
17	Ms. Thomson:	Really? When?
18	Jack:	A couple of weeks ago.
19	Ms. Thomson:	Who said it to whom?
20	Jack:	My dad said it to my mom.
21	Ms. Thomson:	What was the situation?
22	Jack:	My dad went to play golf, but he came home early because of the weather.
23	Ms. Thomson:	So, what do you think it meant?
24	Jack:	I'm not sure. All I know is that it has something to do with rain.
25	Ms. Thomson:	Well, you are definitely right about that. A rain check is a re-entry ticket for a cancelled event because of bad weather.
26	Tiffany:	Do you get to use the ticket on another day?
27	Ms. Thomson:	Yes, you can use the ticket later.
28	Tiffany:	Can we get a rain check for class today since it's raining out?
29	Ms. Thomson:	I am afraid not. Now, let's talk about your family members. Who wants to go first?
30	Joe:	Excuse me, are we allowed to ask the presenters our own questions?
31	Ms. Thomson:	Of course. Please feel free to ask questions to anyone. Alright, Jack, would you care to start?
32	Jack:	Sure. There are four members in my family. Dad, Mom, my sister, and myself.

33	Jane:	How old is your sister, Jack?
34	Jack:	She is ten.
35	Jane:	Which school does she go to?
36	Jack:	She goes to Valley Park Elementary School.
37	Joe:	What does your father do?
38	Jack:	My dad is a teacher.
39	Joe:	What does he teach?
40	Jack:	He teaches math at Fairview High School.
41	Joe:	You must be good at math.
42	Jack:	Kind of. I like math. It's my favorite subject.
43	Tiffany:	What does your mom do?
44	Jack:	She is a nurse.
45	Tiffany:	Where does she work?
46	Jack:	She is working for St. Joseph Hospital in Superior.
47	Ms. Thomson:	Excellent. Now, Jane, can you introduce your family to us?
48	Jane:	Sure. I live with my mom and dad, and I am an only child. My grandparents also live nearby.
49	Tiffany:	How often do you visit them?
50	Jane:	About once a month. They visit us often too.
51	Ms. Thomson:	Excellent. Now, for the remaining time, let's have a group session. Let's divide the class into two groups of four.
52	Ms. Thomson:	Once you get into your groups, ask each other about his or her family.

SKIT 4

WHAT TIME IS DAD GETTING HOME TODAY?

2	Mom:	Tim!
3	Tim:	Yeah?
4	Mom:	Where are you?
5	Tim:	I'm in my room.
6	Mom:	Do you want something to eat?
7	Tim:	Sure.
8	Mom:	(comes in with a tray of food) Here, eat something. What are you up to?
9	Tim:	Just building things with my legos.
10	Mom:	That's impressive! Is that a ship?
11	Tim:	Yep, it's a ship.
12	Mom:	What's her name?
13	Tim:	Tim Ocean. I named her after me.
14	Mom:	I like that name.
15	Tim:	I'm making it for Dad's birthday. So, don't tell him, okay?
16	Mom:	I promise. I'm sure Dad will love it. How long do you think it will take?

17	Tim:	I'm not sure. Maybe two hours or so?
18	Mom:	Two hours? What time will that be?
19	Tim:	Well, what time is it now?
20	Mom:	It's half past three.
21	Tim:	Okay, I think I can finish it by five thirty. Mom?
22	Mom:	Hmm?
23	Tim:	What time is Dad getting home today?
24	Mom:	Around six, as usual.
25	Tim:	Perfect! I'll be done with this just before he gets home.
26	Mom:	What are you going to do after that?
27	Tim:	Can we catch a movie after dinner?
28	Mom:	Sure. What movie?
29	Tim:	Batman. There's a showing at seven thirty and another at nine thirty.
30	Mom:	Nine thirty is too late but the seven thirty showing will work. We'll eat at six thirty.
31	Tim:	Mom?
32	Mom:	Yes?
33	Tim:	What time are we getting up tomorrow to go to the airport?
34	Mom:	We leave at seven, so at six twenty at the latest.
35	Tim:	Why are we leaving so early?
36	Mom:	It takes an hour and a half to get to the airport.
37	Tim:	When's the flight?
38	Mom:	Nine forty five.
39	Tim:	How long does it take to go to Grandma's?
40	Mom:	A little over two hours.
41	Tim:	That's it?
42	Mom:	Well it takes another half hour from the airport to Grandma's house.

43	Tim:	What time will we get there then?
44	Mom:	Probably around a quarter till two. Chicago is an hour ahead of us.
45	Tim:	When are we getting back?
46	Mom:	We'll be back in Denver around quarter to five in the afternoon on Sunday.
47	Tim:	So, we'll be home around six thirty?
48	Mom:	Yeah, that sounds about right.

SKIT 5

WHEN IS DAD'S BIRTHDAY?

2	Tina:	Mom?
3	Mom:	Yeah?
4	Tina:	Can I go to Michelle's birthday party?
5	Mom:	Oh, did she invite you?
6	Tina:	Yeah, she did.
7	Mom:	Sure! When is it?
8	Tina:	Next Saturday.
9	Mom:	What time?
10	Tina:	Two thirty.
11	Mom:	Do you know where the party is?
12	Tina:	Yea, it's at the recreation center by her house.
13	Mom:	Great! Do you need to bring anything?
14	Tina:	She told me to bring my swimsuit.
15	Mom:	All right. When is her birthday?
16	Tina:	March twenty second (March 22nd).
17	Mom:	Oh, okay. What do you want to buy her?
18	Tina:	I'm not sure. She didn't tell me what she wanted. Should I ask her?
19	Mom:	You can call her later.
20	Tina:	I'll just ask her tomorrow at school.

21	Mom:	Good idea.
22	Tina:	Mom, when's your birthday?
23	Mom:	You forgot?
24	Tina:	Sorry, I only remember mine!
25	Mom:	Oh Tina…
26	Tina:	So when is it?
27	Mom:	It's the seventeenth of June (17th of June), nineteen seventy six (1976).
28	Tina:	How old are you?
29	Mom:	We can do the math together.
30	Tina:	Okay. What year is it?
31	Mom:	It's two thousand twelve (2012).
32	Tina:	So I should subtract two thousand twelve (2012) from one thousand nine hundred and seventy six (1976)?
33	Mom:	No, no, it's the other way around.
34	Tina:	So two thousand twelve (2012) minus a thousand nine hundred seventy six (1976), right?
35	Mom:	Yeah that's right!
36	Tina:	(does the math) I got thirty six (36)!
37	Mom:	Good, Tina! You're right! I'm thirty six (36).
38	Tina:	Wow, you're so old… Where's Tim?
39	Mom:	He's at the park with his friends.
40	Tina:	When is his birthday?
41	Mom:	His birthday's the twenty seventh of February (27th of February), two thousand four (2004).
42	Tina:	That's easy! So he's eight years old!
43	Mom:	There you go. He's two years older than you.
44	Tina:	When's Dad's birthday?
45	Mom:	Dad's birthday is March sixth (March 6th), nineteen seventy seven (1977).

46	Tina:	So you were born in nineteen seventy six (1976) and he was born in nineteen seventy seven (1977)?
47	Mom:	That's right! Daddy is one year younger than me.
48	Tina:	It's so fun figuring out people's ages!
49	Mom:	Really?
50	Tina:	Yeah! When's Grandma's birthday?
51	Mom:	Which grandma?
52	Tina:	The one in Denver!
53	Mom:	Her birthday is the ninth of September (9th of September), nineteen forty eight (1948).
54	Tina:	How old is she?
55	Mom:	Do the math again!
56	Tina:	Okay. (does the math) Is she sixty four?
57	Mom:	Yes. Yes indeed!
58	Tina:	What about the grandma in Oregon? When is her birthday?
59	Mom:	Hers is the fifteenth of August (15th of August), and I think she was born in nineteen forty three (1943).
60	Tina:	I see, so she's five years older than Denver Grandma.
61	Mom:	That's right! Very good.
62	Tina:	I want to know how old my grandpas are too!
63	Mom:	Denver Grandpa's birthday is June eighteenth (June 18th), nineteen forty five (1945).
64	Tina:	Okay hold on. I'm going to figure out how old he is.
65	Mom:	Alright, take your time.
66	Tina:	He's sixty seven!
67	Mom:	Good job! You're getting faster and faster!
68	Tina:	When's Oregon Grandpa's birthday?

69	Mom:	His birthday's November eleventh (November 11th), nineteen forty three (1943).
70	Tina:	Isn't Oregon Grandma's birthday in nineteen forty three (1943), too?
71	Mom:	Yeah, it is.
72	Tina:	So they're both sixty nine!
73	Mom:	Yep! You're a genius, Tina!
74	Tina:	Now I know everyone's birthdays in my family!

SKIT 6

CAN WE TALK ABOUT PETS?

2	Mom:	Hey, sweetie! How was school today?
3	Tina:	It was okay.
4	Mom:	That doesn't sound too good. What happened?
5	Tina:	Nothing.
6	Mom:	You sure?
7	Tina:	Yeah I just didn't like the lunch.
8	Mom:	What was for lunch?
9	Tina:	Chicken.
10	Mom:	What was wrong with it?
11	Tina:	It was gross.
12	Mom:	That's it?
13	Tina:	Yeah.
14	Mom:	I see. Well, let's go home.
15	Tina:	Mom?
16	Mom:	Yes?
17	Tina:	Can we stop by the grocery store on our way home?
18	Mom:	Why? Do you want something to eat?
19	Tina:	Yeah, I want some ice cream.
20	Mom:	You do realize that you've been having ice cream everyday for the past week, right?

21	Tina:	Yeah. Is it bad to have it everyday?
22	Mom:	Of course. Eating anything with too much artificial flavoring and sugar everyday is bad.
23	Tina:	Oh okay…
24	Mom:	Do you have homework?
25	Tina:	Yeah, my teacher said to talk to our parents about animals.
26	Mom:	Animals?
27	Tina:	Yeah, animals you can have as pets!
28	Mom:	Hmm, interesting. Do you have any other homework?
29	Tina:	I do have some reading to do.
30	Mom:	Do the reading first, then we'll talk about pets after dinner.
31	Tina:	That's what I was going to do.
32	Mom:	Perfect!
33	Note:	(after dinner)
34	Tina:	Dad?
35	Dad:	Yes, princess?
36	Tina:	Can we talk about pets?
37	Dad:	Is this for homework?
38	Tina:	Yes.
39	Dad:	Okay, sure. Start by listing animals people can have as pets.
40	Tina:	Dogs!
41	Mom:	That's right! Many people have dogs because they're very smart and loyal to their owners.
42	Dad:	Exactly.
43	Tina:	Can we have a dog?
44	Mom:	We can discuss that later!

45	Dad:	Yes, we can discuss that later. What other animals can you think of?
46	Tina:	A cat?
47	Mom:	Yes, of course!
48	Dad:	Many people do indeed have cats as pets!
49	Tina:	I want a cat too!
50	Dad:	Tina, I don't think we can have a cat and a dog.
51	Tina:	It would be so much fun to have both though!
52	Mom:	I know, I know, but taking care of them would take so much time and effort.
53	Tina:	But all of my friends have a cat or a dog!
54	Dad:	I understand, but we can't afford to have a pet!
55	Mom:	Sorry, sweetie, maybe you can have both when you grow up!
56	Tina:	Okay.
57	Mom:	Good girl. Now what other animals can people have as pets?
58	Tina:	How about rabbits?
59	Dad:	Rabbits?
60	Tina:	Yeah! People have rabbits, don't they?
61	Mom:	They do!
62	Dad:	I don't think so...
63	Mom:	Of course people do, Honey.
64	Tina:	What about snakes?
65	Dad:	Oh yeah, I know a few people who absolutely love snakes.
66	Mom:	I don't like snakes...small snakes, big snakes, colorful snakes--I hate them all. They're gross!
67	Dad:	Yeah, I don't like snakes either.
68	Tina:	Dad, what other animals do people keep as pets?
69	Dad:	A cow!

70	Mom:	Hon, that's not exactly a pet.
71	Tina:	Oh, what about a horse?
72	Mom:	That's not a pet either! Those are animals raised on a farm.
73	Tina:	Oh, okay.
74	Tina:	What about roosters?
75	Dad:	Those are also raised outside on a farm! Well, in chicken coops.
76	Tina:	How about a tiger? Can you have a tiger for a pet?
77	Mom:	I don't think so.
78	Dad:	I've never heard of anyone raising a tiger.
79	Tina:	What about monkeys?
80	Mom:	Probably not. Those are animals at the zoo for people to see when they want!
81	Tina:	I saw all kinds of animals there last year!
82	Dad:	I bet you did! We can go to the zoo this weekend, if you would like to.
83	Tina:	Really?
84	Dad:	Of course.
85	Tina:	Thanks Dad.
86	Dad:	Anything for my girl.
87	Mom:	Is that it for your homework?
88	Tina:	I think so. Thanks for helping me!
89	Dad:	Sure. Any time.
90	Mom:	I'm glad I could be of help.

Skit 7

I DON'T WANT TO GET UP.

2	Note:	(Part 1: Mom wakes Tina up)
3	Mom:	Tina! Good morning!
4	Tina:	Good morning. I don't want to get up.
5	Mom:	Why not?
6	Tina:	I just don't feel like it.
7	Mom:	Did you not sleep well?
8	Tina:	I don't know. I had a dream though.
9	Mom:	Oh, sweetie, was it a nightmare?
10	Tina:	Nope.
11	Mom:	Oh, okay. What was it about?
12	Tina:	My friends were in it.
13	Mom:	Who?
14	Tina:	I didn't know them.
15	Mom:	Oh, really?
16	Tina:	Yeah. But they were nice.
17	Mom:	What did you guys do?
18	Tina:	I don't remember.
19	Mom:	It's okay, I never remember my dreams either.
20	Tina:	What time is it?
21	Mom:	It's a quarter till seven.

22	Tina:	Mom?
23	Mom:	Yes?
24	Tina:	How's the weather?
25	Mom:	It's sunny! I'll open the curtains.
26	Tina:	Is it Wednesday?
27	Mom:	It's Tuesday. You have swim lessons on Mondays and you had a lesson yesterday, remember?
28	Tina:	Oh, yeah. I remember.
29	Mom:	Good, good. Are you ready to get up now?
30	Tina:	Yeah. What's for breakfast?
31	Mom:	That's up to you! What do you want?
32	Tina:	Cereal in milk!
33	Mom:	Sounds good. Make your bed and get ready while I get that ready for you.
34	Tina:	Okay!
35	Mom:	Good girl. I love you, sweetie.
36	Tina:	What should I wear?
37	Mom:	Anything you want.
38	Tina:	Which pants, Mom?
39	Mom:	The yellow ones look good, sweetie.
40	Tina:	Okay.
41	Mom:	I'll be in the kitchen. Come down once you wash up and dress!
42	Tina:	Okay. Is Tim up yet?
43	Mom:	I think so. Dad's in his room now.
44	Note:	(Part 2: Dad in Tim's room)
45	Dad:	Good morning, Son! Time to get up. The sun has risen.
46	Tim:	Good morning, Dad!
47	Dad:	Did you sleep well?
48	Tim:	Not really.

49	Dad:	Why not?
50	Tim:	There were sirens going off all night.
51	Dad:	Oh, I didn't hear anything.
52	Tim:	Yeah, they woke me up a few times.
53	Dad:	Huh, I must've been in a deep sleep.
54	Tim:	Dad?
55	Dad:	Yeah?
56	Tim:	Can I get a phone?
57	Dad:	A phone?
58	Tim:	Yeah.
59	Dad:	I'll talk to Mom about it. In the meantime, get dressed and come down for breakfast.
60	Tim:	Thanks, Dad.
61	Dad:	I'm going to open the windows to freshen up the air.
62	Tim:	Do you know what's for breakfast?
63	Dad:	Nope, we'll see.
64	Tim:	I hope it isn't cereal in milk...
65	Dad:	Why?
66	Tim:	Because we have that every morning.
67	Dad:	It's still good though.
68	Tim:	I know, but I want something different.
69	Dad:	We can talk to Mom about it.
70	Tim:	Dad, can you give me a ride to school?
71	Dad:	What's wrong with the bus?
72	Tim:	I don't want to walk to the bus stop.
73	Dad:	I don't think that's a good reason to ask for a ride.
74	Tim:	Can I bike to the stop then?
75	Dad:	It's only 300 yards! Besides, you should get a little bit of exercise everyday anyway!
76	Tim:	Okay.

77	Dad:	Alright, get up and make your bed now.
78	Tim:	Okay.
79	Dad:	(as he is walking out of the room) And get ready for school after that!
80	Note:	(Part 3: Kids getting dressed)
81	Tim:	(in his room) Mom!
82	Mom:	Yes?
83	Tim:	Where are my socks?
84	Mom:	They should be in the small drawer.
85	Tim:	There aren't any in the small drawer!
86	Mom:	(to husband), Honey!
87	Dad:	What's up?
88	Mom:	Can you get Tim a pair of socks from the laundry room, please?
89	Dad:	Of course.
90	Mom:	Thank you!
91	Dad:	Sure thing.
92	Tina:	(in her room) Mom!
93	Mom:	What now?
94	Tina:	I can't find my hair band!
95	Mom:	Look around.
96	Tina:	Ok, I found it. Never mind, Mom.
97	Tim:	Where is my shirt?
98	Mom:	I'm busy making breakfast. Ask Dad.
99	Dad:	What are you looking for?
100	Tim:	My shirt!
101	Dad:	Which one?
102	Tim:	The one with cars on it.
103	Dad:	Oh I think I saw it in the dryer.
104	Tim:	Right, I'll go get it.
105	Mom:	Breakfast is ready!

106	Dad:	Let's go eat.
107	Tim:	Okay, I'll be there soon after I get my shirt!
108	Dad:	Okay. Hurry, please.
109	Note:	(Part 4: At the breakfast table)
110	Tim:	Mom!
111	Mom:	Yeah?
112	Tim:	Can I get some apple juice?
113	Mom:	You don't like milk?
114	Tim:	Not today.
115	Mom:	Okay, I will get you some apple juice. Here you go.
116	Tim:	Thanks, Mom.
117	Mom:	Any time.
118	Tina:	I like milk in the morning. It's refreshing.
119	Dad:	Good, I'm glad you like milk in the morning but you should have some fruit too, Tina. You too, Tim.
120	Tim:	I will.
121	Tina:	Mom!
122	Mom:	Yes, sweetie?
123	Tina:	What's for lunch?
124	Mom:	Just buy lunch at school today.
125	Tina:	Oh, okay.
126	Dad:	What time does school end today, kids?
127	Tina:	Dad, you always ask the same question!
128	Tim:	Honestly. It ends at two thirty everyday.
129	Dad:	(laughs) What are you guys doing after school today?
130	Tina:	You ask that every morning too.
131	Mom:	But you guys don't do the same thing after school everyday.

132	Dad:	Exactly.
133	Tina:	I'm going to hang out with some friends.
134	Tim:	Me too.
135	Dad:	What are you going to do with them?
136	Tina:	We don't know. Just go out.
137	Tim:	I think we're going to go biking for a while.
138	Dad:	Alright, sounds good! I'm glad you chose that over video games!
139	Tim:	Why don't you want us playing video games?
140	Mom:	It's a lot healthier to be playing outside!
141	Dad:	Most definitely.
142	Mom:	Alright kids, it's time to go catch your school bus!
143	Dad:	Go brush your teeth and get your backpacks.
144	Tina:	(leaving home for school) Bye, Mom! Bye, Dad!
145	Tim:	Bye!
146	Dad:	Have fun!
147	Mom:	Wait, wait! I'll walk you to the bus stop.
148	Tina:	Okay!
149	Tim:	Okay.
150	Dad:	Okay, well I need to get going.
151	Mom:	Alright, bye! See you tonight!

SKIT 8

AFTER SCHOOL

2	Tim:	(Tim comes home) Mom, I'm home!
3	Mom:	Hi, sweetie! How was your day?
4	Tim:	It was good!
5	Mom:	That's good to hear.
6	Tim:	Can I get something to eat?
7	Mom:	Are you hungry?
8	Tim:	No. I just want something to eat.
9	Mom:	How was the lunch today?
10	Tim:	It was okay. Chicken nuggets and salad.
11	Mom:	That doesn't sound too bad. Well, I will go bake some potatoes right now.
12	Tim:	Can I have some ice cream instead?
13	Mom:	Sorry, sweetie. We ran out.
14	Tim:	Oh, can Dad get some on his way home?
15	Mom:	You can ask him.
16	Tim:	Okay. I'll call him. What time is it now?
17	Mom:	It's almost four. He should be in his office.
18	Note:	(Tim calls Dad)
19	Dad:	Hey, Tim!
20	Tim:	When are you getting home today?
21	Dad:	Around six, why?

22	Tim:	Could you stop by the grocery store and buy some ice cream on the way home?
23	Dad:	I don't see why not.
24	Tim:	Thanks, Dad!
25	Dad:	Sure, see you later.
26	Mom:	What did he say?
27	Tim:	He said he will buy some on the way home!
28	Mom:	Oh, how nice of him!
29	Tina:	(gets home) I'm home!
30	Mom:	How was school, sweetie?
31	Tina:	Not bad.
32	Mom:	Did something happen?
33	Tina:	No, not really.
34	Mom:	You look down.
35	Tina:	I'm just tired.
36	Mom:	Okay. Do you want some baked potatoes?
37	Tina:	Yes! I love baked potatoes!
38	Mom:	I know you do! They'll be ready in just a few minutes.
39	Tina:	Okay.
40	Tim:	Guess what?!
41	Tina:	What?
42	Tim:	I called Dad and he's buying ice cream on his way home today.
43	Tina:	Great! What kind?
44	Tim:	I don't know but probably cookies and cream as usual.
45	Tina:	That's my favorite!
46	Tim:	Mine too. Chocolate ice cream is good too.
47	Tim:	Mom!
48	Mom:	Yes, Honey?

49	Tim:	Can I go play video games?
50	Mom:	No, how about you go read instead?
51	Tim:	Can I play some video games afterwards?
52	Mom:	I don't think you'll have time to play video games after you finish reading. You have piano, remember?
53	Tina:	Tim, don't you remember what Dad said?
54	Tim:	What?
55	Tina:	He said it's not healthy to play video games all the time.
56	Tim:	I know.
57	Mom:	The potatoes are ready! Come eat!
58	Kids:	Coming!
59	Note:	(at the table)
60	Tina:	Could you pass the cheese, Mom?
61	Mom:	Sure.
62	Tim:	Tina, can you pass me the salt?
63	Tina:	Here you go.
64	Tim:	Thanks.
65	Mom:	Do you have homework today?
66	Tina:	Yes, but not much.
67	Tim:	Same here.
68	Mom:	Go out and play with some friends after you eat, okay?
69	Tim:	Mom, can I go to Kevin's?
70	Mom:	Of course. Remember to behave yourself, okay?
71	Tim:	Don't worry, Mom. I'm not a baby.
72	Mom:	Tina, what about you?
73	Tina:	I'm going to go biking.
74	Mom:	Be careful and make sure you have your helmet on.
75	Tina:	I will. What time should I be back by?

76	Mom:	Six. Also, make sure you close the door all the way when you go out.
77	Kids:	Okay.
78	Tim:	By the way, what's for dinner?
79	Mom:	Chicken soup.
80	Tim:	Delicious. I'm done with my potato. See you later!
81	Mom:	Okay.
82	Tina:	I'm ready too! Bye!
83	Mom:	Bye.
84	Note:	(after a while)
85	Dad:	Honey, I am home!
86	Mom:	Hey, Honey! You're early today!
87	Dad:	Yeah, my field meeting was cancelled.
88	Mom:	Oh good. How was work today?
89	Dad:	Great! Great!
90	Mom:	You always say 'Great!'
91	Dad:	Because I like it when it's great. How about you?
92	Mom:	I'm a bit tired. I had some issues at work.
93	Dad:	Relax, Honey. Don't let them bother you.
94	Mom:	Thanks, Honey. I like how you handle things like that.
95	Dad:	I'm flattered.
96	Tim:	I'm home, Mom!
97	Dad:	Hello!
98	Tim:	Hey, Dad! Did you get the ice cream?
99	Dad:	What do you think?
100	Tim:	You got it?
101	Dad:	Of course. Who do you think I am?
102	Tim:	You're my dad!
103	Dad:	That's right!
104	Tina:	I'm back, Mom! Hi, Dad!

105	Dad:	Hi, sweetie!
106	Tim:	I'm hungry!
107	Mom:	I know. Dinner will be ready soon.
108	Dad:	How'd you do in school, kids?
109	Tim:	I did alright.
110	Tina:	I did alright as well.
111	Mom:	Could you set the table, please?
112	Dad:	Of course!
113	Mom:	Thanks, Honey.
114	Dad:	Any time.
115	Mom:	Dinner's ready!
116	Kids:	Coming!
117	Dad:	Did you kids wash your hands?
118	Kids:	No. Not yet.
119	Dad:	Please go wash your hands.
120	Kids:	Okay.
121	Tim:	Chicken soup! My favorite.
122	Tina:	Could you please pass the salt and pepper?
123	Mom:	Of course. Here you go.
124	Tina:	Thanks, Mom.
125	Mom:	You're welcome.
126	Dad:	This is really good. You're a great cook.
127	Mom:	Thanks! Help yourself.
128	Tim:	I wish the soup wasn't so hot.
129	Dad:	Blow on it before putting it in your mouth. That should help.
130	Mom:	Also, eating fast is not a good habit.
131	Tim:	Okay. Is there enough for seconds?
132	Mom:	Of course.
133	Note:	(after dinner)
134	Tim:	Thanks for the dinner, Mom. It was really good.

135	Mom:	Of course sweetie, I'm glad to hear that.
136	Tina:	I enjoyed the dinner, too. Thanks, Mom.
137	Mom:	Thanks, sweetie.
138	Tim:	Can we have ice cream for dessert?
139	Mom:	Sure.
140	Tina:	Yes! I'll get it. Where is the ice cream, Mom?
141	Mom:	It's in the freezer.
142	Tim:	I'll get the scooper. Where's the scooper, Mom?
143	Mom:	It should be in the silverware drawer.
144	Tim:	Dad, how much do you want?
145	Dad:	Two scoops, please.
146	Tim:	How about you, Mom?
147	Mom:	Same here.
148	Tim:	Okay. What about you, Tina?
149	Tina:	I'll get mine myself.
150	Tim:	Okay. I will take five scoops.
151	Dad:	That's a little too much, Tim.
152	Tim:	Four scoops? (Dad nods)
153	Dad:	Kids, are you done with homework yet?
154	Tina:	Not yet, but I don't have much. It shouldn't take long.
155	Tim:	Me neither. I will do it soon.
156	Dad:	Sounds good.
157	Mom:	Take a shower before you start your homework, alright?
158	Kids:	Alright.
159	Dad:	Brush your teeth while you're at it!
160	Tim:	I will.
161	Tina:	Yes, Dad.
162	Mom:	Remember to put your dirty clothes in the laundry basket as well.

163	Tim:	I know.
164	Tina:	Yes, Mom.
165	Dad:	Do either one of you need help with homework?
166	Tim:	No, I don't think so. I just need to do some reading.
167	Tina:	I'm fine. I'll let you know if I need help, though.
168	Dad:	Good!
169	Tim:	I'm done eating. I'll shower first.
170	Dad:	Kids, could you please take your dishes to the sink?
171	Tina:	Okay.
172	Dad:	Thanks. That helps a lot.

Skit 9

RAINY AFTERNOON

2	Mom:	Tina!
3	Tina:	(from her room) Yeah?
4	Mom:	Could you do me a favor?
5	Tina:	(coming out of her room) Sure. What do you need help with?
6	Mom:	Could you close the windows? It looks like it's going to rain any minute now.
7	Tina:	Yes, of course.
8	Mom:	Thanks, sweetie.
9	Tina:	(after closing windows) Where's Dad, Mom?
10	Mom:	He's still at work. He said he will be coming in late tonight.
11	Tina:	Mom! It's raining!
12	Mom:	Yeah, looks like we'll have a lot of rain.
13	Tina:	What did the weather forecast say today?
14	Mom:	They said we will have heavy rain tonight.
15	Tina:	Will it rain tomorrow too?
16	Mom:	I'm afraid so.
17	Tina:	I don't like wearing rain coats. They're too stuffy.
18	Mom:	Yeah. It's better than getting wet though!

19	Tina:	They're really uncomfortable, too.
20	Mom:	I know sweetie. You like them better than umbrellas though, right?
21	Tina:	Yes, I do.
22	Mom:	Can you go get Tim?
23	Tina:	Where did he go?
24	Mom:	He went to the park.
25	Tina:	Okay, I'll go get him.
26	Tim:	I'm home!
27	Tina:	Perfect timing! I was just about to go out and get you.
28	Mom:	Hey, sweetie! Oh good, you aren't wet. Go wash your hands.
29	Tim:	Okay. Can I have something to eat afterwards?
30	Mom:	Sure. There are oranges on the table.
31	Tina:	I like snow much more than rain.
32	Mom:	I do too but I think the temperature outside is unbearable when it starts snowing. Don't you agree?
33	Tina:	Yeah, but you can play in it! You can go skiing and sledding!
34	Mom:	I don't like either of them. I like seasons without snow or rain.
35	Tina:	Like spring and fall?
36	Mom:	Yeah. Exactly.
37	Tina:	But it gets really windy in the spring.
38	Mom:	I know, but I can deal with wind.
39	Tim:	(from the bathroom) Mom! The toilet is clogged!
40	Mom:	Don't worry and stop flushing it.
41	Tim:	Okay.

42	Mom:	When you clog up the toilet, stop flushing. Just let me or Dad know and we'll take care of it, alright?
43	Tim:	Okay. Oh, the shower head is leaking as well.
44	Mom:	Yes I know. Dad will fix it when he has time.
45	Tim:	Can Dad really fix anything, Mom?
46	Mom:	Dad can do a lot of things.
47	Tim:	Can he fix everything in the house?
48	Mom:	Pretty much. He can fix most of the home appliances like the washer, dryer, freezer, oven and things like that.
49	Tim:	He fixed my bike, too.
50	Tina:	And mine!
51	Mom:	Not everyone can do that like your Dad.
52	Tina:	We're so lucky to have a handyman like Dad.
53	Tim:	What is he not good at?
54	Mom:	I know one thing.
55	Tina:	What is it?
56	Mom:	This is a secret between us, okay?
57	Kids:	Yes, Mom. What is it?
58	Mom:	Your dad cannot sing.
59	Tina:	What? Really?
60	Tim:	Are you serious?
61	Mom:	Yes. Dead serious. Have you ever heard him sing?
62	Tina:	Come to think of it, no, I haven't.
63	Tim:	Me neither.
64	Mom:	See?
65	Tina:	I still like Dad a lot.
66	Tim:	I love him a lot, too.
67	Mom:	I love your dad a lot too.
68	Tina:	Look! It's pouring outside!

69   Mom: Yes it is! I need to start preparing dinner. So will you guys go upstairs and clean your rooms in the meantime?

70   Kids: Sure. We will.

Skit 10

WEEKEND SHOPPING

2	Dad:	Tim! Tina! We are going grocery shopping!
3	Tim:	Where are we going grocery shopping, Dad?
4	Dad:	We are going to Costco.
5	Tim:	Are we going out for lunch afterwards?
6	Dad:	Of course.
7	Tim:	Great! I love eating out!
8	Dad:	Yes, you sure do!
9	Tina:	Are you going to buy me anything?
10	Dad:	Of course, what do you want?
11	Tina:	I want to buy hairbands.
12	Dad:	You got it.
13	Mom:	Didn't you buy hairbands last time?
14	Tina:	Yeah, but I want different ones!
15	Dad:	Okay, get ready. We're leaving in ten minutes.
16	Kids:	Okay, Daddy.
17	Mom:	It's really nice out today.
18	Dad:	Yea, it is. It couldn't be better.
19	Mom:	Where should we go for lunch?
20	Dad:	I've no idea. Do you have a restaurant in mind?
21	Mom:	No, but can we go for some Italian food since the kids love it so much.

22	Dad:	That sounds good to me.
23	Kids:	We're ready!
24	Dad:	Okay, kids. Let's hit the road.
25	Tim:	Which car are we going in?
26	Dad:	Let's go in mine.
27	Tina:	Yeah, I like Dad's car.
28	Mom:	Why is that, Tina?
29	Tim:	I know why!
30	Mom:	Why?
31	Tim:	Dad always has something to eat in his car. Right, Tina?
32	Tina:	Yes.
33	Mom:	Like what?
34	Tina:	Candy, chocolate, gum, things like that!
35	Dad:	Okay, kids. Here we go!
36	Mom:	Hey Tina?
37	Tina:	Yeah, Mom?
38	Mom:	How many hairbands do you want to buy?
39	Tina:	I want at least 10 of them.
40	Mom:	Wow, that seems like a few too many.
41	Tina:	Mom, ten is not too many.
42	Mom:	Alright, if you say so. Do you have a price estimate?
43	Tina:	No.
44	Mom:	I guess we'll have to see when we get there.
45	Note:	(after a while)
46	Dad:	Here we are, everybody.
47	Mom:	Tim, can you grab a cart, please?
48	Tim:	Sure, Mom.
49	Tina:	Dad?
50	Dad:	Yes, Tina?

51	Tina:	What do we need to buy?
52	Dad:	You should ask Mom that.
53	Tina:	Okay. Mom?
54	Mom:	Yes, sweetie?
55	Tina:	What do we need to buy?
56	Mom:	We need to buy some meat, vegetables, fruit, and fish.
57	Tim:	Oh, I love meat! Let's buy beef, pork, AND chicken!
58	Dad:	We can buy a little bit of each.
59	Tina:	I like vegetables more than meat.
60	Mom:	I know you do.
61	Dad:	I know that too! We should buy some carrots, potatoes, sweet potatoes, cucumbers, squash, and zucchini.
62	Mom:	Don't forget that we need some lettuce, spinach, and celery.
63	Tina:	Mommy, don't forget the fruits!
64	Mom:	I won't! We can grab some apples, pears and oranges.
65	Tim:	What about fish?
66	Dad:	I would like to have some fluke and salmon.
67	Tim:	I love fluke sashimi.
68	Tina:	I like trout sashimi better.
69	Mom:	Me too. The trout Dad caught at the lake a few weeks ago were really good.
70	Dad:	Were they? I'll go fishing next Saturday and bring back some more then!
71	Tim:	Can I go with you?
72	Dad:	Sure, you are always welcome.
73	Tina:	I don't like going there.
74	Dad:	Why not, Tina?

75	Tina:	It's too far.
76	Dad:	That's it?
77	Tina:	And there's no place to play.
78	Dad:	Okay. You can stay home with Mommy then.
79	Tina:	Mom?
80	Mom:	Yes, sweetie?
81	Tina:	Can we get some ice cream?
82	Mom:	Sure, what flavor do you want?
83	Tina:	That cookies and cream one over there.
84	Mom:	Okay. I will get it for you.
85	Dad:	Honey, did we get everything we need?
86	Mom:	I think so.
87	Dad:	Alright, let's go checkout then!
88	Tina:	Can I ride on the cart?
89	Dad:	No, you're too big to ride on the cart now
90	Tina:	Okay.
91	Dad:	Good girl.
92	Note:	(at the cashier)
93	Cashier:	Good morning!
94	Dad:	Good morning!
95	Cashier:	How are you folks doing today?
96	Dad:	Good! We're good, thanks! How are you?
97	Cashier:	Fine, thank you. Did you find everything alright?
98	Dad:	Yes, we did!
99	Cashier:	Would you like plastic or paper bags?
100	Dad:	Paper, please.
101	Cashier:	Of course.
102	Note:	(after tallying everything up)
103	Cashier:	Anything else?
104	Dad:	Nope, that will be it!
105	Cashier:	Your total is one thirty four fifty six ($134.56).

106	Mom:	Honey, you can use Amex.
107	Dad:	Okay. Do you take American Express?
108	Cashier:	We sure do! Go ahead and slide it right through that card machine over there.
109	Dad:	Okay (slides the card).
110	Cashier:	Oops. Sorry, the card didn't go through. Could you slide it once again please?
111	Dad:	Huh, that's strange (slides card again).
112	Cashier:	Nope, it isn't going through. Can I look at the card?
113	Tim:	Mom, what's wrong?
114	Mom:	Nothing. Just wait.
115	Dad:	Sure, here you go.
116	Cashier:	Thanks. Oh, I see. The Costco membership was expired as of yesterday.
117	Dad:	Oh, really? I didn't realize. Please include the membership fee, then.
118	Cashier:	Sure.
119	Dad:	(After sign) Okay.
120	Cashier:	Thanks.
121	Dad:	Of course.
122	Cashier:	Thanks. You are all set. Have a nice one.
123	Dad:	You too.

TALKING ABOUT SCHOOL

2	Dad:	How's school these days, Tim?
3	Tim:	I like it very much, Dad.
4	Dad:	I am glad to hear that.
5	Mom:	Tim aced his science and math quiz today!
6	Dad:	Wow! Great job! High five!
7	Tim:	I didn't ace English though.
8	Dad:	What did you get in English?
9	Tim:	I got a B-.
10	Dad:	That's not bad at all, son!
11	Mom:	He could have done better if he studied a little more last night.
12	Dad:	Don't worry! I'm happy with what he got.
13	Tim:	Thanks, Dad.
14	Dad:	No problem. How are your friends?
15	Tim:	They are all good.
16	Dad:	Don't you get tired during first period?
17	Tim:	A little bit.
18	Mom:	See? You should listen to me when I tell you to go to bed a little earlier!
19	Dad:	What about second period?

20	Tim:	Everybody is up because Ms. Myers is very fun. She is a very good teacher.
21	Mom:	It sounds like everybody really likes her.
22	Tim:	Yes, everyone really does.
23	Dad:	Do any of your friends pick on you?
24	Tim:	No.
25	Dad:	Do you see any students bullying other kids?
26	Tim:	I haven't seen anything like that yet.
27	Dad:	I'm glad you're doing just fine at school.
28	Mom:	Me too. Treat the others the way you want to be treated, alright, Tim?
29	Tim:	I always treat everyone well.
30	Dad:	Good. If anyone bullies you, tell the teacher.
31	Tim:	I will, Dad.
32	Mom:	Also, let us know. Will you, Tim?
33	Tim:	Yes, Mom.
34	Dad:	That's right. We want you to be happy at school.
35	Mom:	So if you have any problems, feel free to talk to us.
36	Tim:	I will, Mom.
37	Dad:	If you see someone in trouble, help him or her.
38	Tim:	Trouble?
39	Dad:	Like if someone is being bullied at school.
40	Tim:	How do I help them?
41	Dad:	You can report the bully to your teacher or the principal.
42	Tim:	What if the bully seeks revenge?
43	Dad:	Don't be afraid! You have me, Mom, your teachers, friends, and many others to help you out.
44	Mom:	If you are really worried about the bully seeking revenge, let your teacher know.
45	Dad:	Let us know as well and we'll help you too.

46	Tim:	I will. By the way, I have a question, Dad.
47	Dad:	What's that?
48	Tim:	Is it okay to share my lunch with other kids?
49	Dad:	I guess it depends.
50	Tim:	On what?
51	Dad:	On what their parents think.
52	Tim:	So, should I or should I not share my lunch with my friends?
53	Dad:	I'll let your mom answer that one.
54	Mom:	I think it's okay if it's every once in a while.
55	Tim:	Why not everyday?
56	Mom:	Your friends' parents may not like it.
57	Tim:	What do you think about other kids sharing their lunches with me?
58	Mom:	I am okay with that. But some kids may be allergic to certain foods that they are not yet aware of.
59	Tim:	I see. Thanks, Mom.
60	Dad:	What do you do during recess?
61	Tim:	I play with my friends.
62	Dad:	That's good. Try to get along with everyone, all right?
63	Tim:	Okay.
64	Mom:	Who's your best friend now?
65	Tim:	The same as usual. Kevin and Daniel.
66	Dad:	What are they good at?
67	Tim:	Kevin's good at math and Daniel's good at science.
68	Dad:	Your favorite class is PE (Physical Education), right?
69	Tim:	Yah, I like gym the most. It's always fun and we don't have homework.
70	Dad:	I used to like gym too, when I was your age.
71	Tim:	Mom, what did you like when you were my age?

72	Mom:	I liked history. Still do. I had a really good teacher so I studied a lot.
73	Dad:	I heard Mom hated math a lot.
74	Tim:	No wonder I hate math.
75	Dad:	But you aced math, didn't you?
76	Tim:	Yes, but that doesn't mean I like it.
77	Dad:	Your mom may not like math, but I loved it and was good at it too!
78	Tim:	So, like parents like son, right, Dad?
79	Dad:	What do you mean? People say "like father like son" or "like mother like daughter," but not "like parents like son."
80	Tim:	I hate math like Mom but I'm good at math like you.
81	Dad:	Oh, I see what you mean.

Skit 12

Q AND A GAME

2	Mr. Myers:	Good morning, everyone! Nice day out, huh?
3	Students:	Yes, Mr. Myers.
4	Mr. Myers:	Today, we are going to play a Q and A game.
5	Tina:	Mr. Myers?
6	Mr. Myers:	Yes, Tina?
7	Tina:	What's a Q and A game?
8	Mr. Myers:	That's a good question. Q stands for question and A stands for answer. So, it's a game of asking questions and answering them!
9	Michelle:	Are we allowed to ask anything?
10	Mr. Myers:	Yes, but within a given subject.
11	Michelle:	What's the subject today?
12	Mr. Myers:	Today's subject is "My Family and Me".
13	Tina:	How do you play a Q and A with that subject?
14	Mr. Myers:	You start by introducing yourself and your family and we will follow up with questions.
15	Michelle:	What do we say about ourselves and our family?
16	Mr. Myers:	Anything. Think about things you would say to a person when you are introducing yourself.

17	Michelle:	My name, birthday, address, phone number, favorite things, Mom, Dad, siblings, pets, and stuff like that.
18	Mr. Myers:	What else can you think of, Tina?
19	Tina:	I don't know.
20	Mr. Myers:	Come on, Tina.
21	Tina:	The name of the school I go to, what grade I'm in, what I do on the weekends, things I like, and things I don't like?
22	Mr. Myers:	Yes! You got it, Tina. Very good.
23	Michelle:	What kinds of questions do we ask the presenter?
24	Mr. Myers:	Anything that will answer what you want to know about them.
25	Tina:	Do I have to answer all questions?
26	Mr. Myers:	Not necessarily, but try to answer as many as you can.
27	Michelle:	What if we don't want to answer a question?
28	Mr. Myers:	Then, just say you don't want to answer.
29	Michelle:	Oh, okay.
30	Mr. Myers:	Now, let me put the things you need to talk about on the board.
31	Note:	(Mr. Myers writes a list on the board)
32	Mr. Myers:	Okay, let's get started. Who would like to start first?
33	Tina:	I'd like to start!
34	Mr. Myers:	Great! Tina, go ahead.
35	Tina:	My name's Tina, I'm nine years old and I'm in second grade, as you know. The name of the school I go to is VSD Elementary School and I really like ice cream.

36	Mr. Myers:	Very good, Tina. Is that all?
37	Tina:	Yes.
38	Mr. Myers:	Great! Let's start asking Tina questions. Michelle?
39	Michelle:	Okay. Tina, where do you live?
40	Tina:	I live by Central Park.
41	Michelle:	What's your address?
42	Tina:	54332 Drew Circle Unit 231, Boulder, CO, and the zip code is 80305.
43	Michelle:	What was the name of the street?
44	Tina:	It's Drew Circle.
45	Michelle:	I am sorry. How do you spell it?
46	Tina:	It's D as in David, R as in rainbow, E as in egg, and W as in white.
47	Michelle:	When's your birthday?
48	Tina:	March sixth, two thousand two.
49	Victor:	Do you have a pet?
50	Tina:	No, I don't. But, my grandparents have a cat, and her name is Lucy.
51	Victor:	What color is Lucy?
52	Tina:	Black and white.
53	Michelle:	What do you like to do on Sundays?
54	Tina:	I like to bike along the creek with my mom and dad.
55	Michelle:	What kind of bike do you have?
56	Tina:	My dad and mom have a tandem bike, and I have a mountain bike.
57	Victor:	What is your least favorite thing to do?
58	Tina:	I don't like cleaning the house. It isn't fun.
59	Victor:	Who cooks in your house?

60	Tina:	Mostly my mom, but my dad cooks once in a while, too.
61	Victor:	Who drives you to school?
62	Tina:	I bike to school.
63	Mr. Myers:	Very good. Now, let's have Victor introduce himself and answer questions.
64	Victor:	Okay. My name is Victor, my last name is Smith. I just turned 9 last Friday. I will answer questions now.
65	Michelle:	What's your favorite season of the year?
66	Victor:	Definitely summer.
67	Michelle:	Why?
68	Victor:	Just because.
69	Tina:	What do you do on weekends?
70	Victor:	I have piano lessons in the morning on Saturdays.
71	Tina:	How long have you played the piano for?
72	Victor:	Since I was 6.
73	Michelle:	Who do you like the most in your family?
74	Victor:	I like everyone but I like my Dad in particular. He's awesome and likes to play with me.
75	Michelle:	Do you have a brother or sister?
76	Victor:	Yes, I have a sister.
77	Michelle:	How old is she?
78	Victor:	She is six years old, but she will turn seven next month.
79	Michelle:	What's her name?
80	Victor:	Her name is Anna.
81	Michelle:	What does she like to do?
82	Victor:	She likes to play with stuffed animals.
83	Michelle:	Does she have a lot of friends?

84	Victor:	Yes, she does. She loves to play with her friends.
85	Tina:	Do you have a phone?
86	Victor:	Yes.
87	Tina:	What's your phone number?
88	Victor:	Three-nine-zero, nine-nine-zero, nine-nine-nine-eight.
89	Tina:	What is your favorite fruit?
90	Victor:	I don't have a favorite, but I do like pears a lot.
91	Tina:	What does your dad do?
92	Victor:	He works for himself. He is an accountant.
93	Tina:	What about your mom?
94	Victor:	My mom works at the city library. She really likes her job.
95	Mr. Myers:	Very good, Victor! Let's move onto Michelle now.
96	Michelle:	My name is Michelle and I live with my parents and sister. We have a dog, too.
97	Victor:	About the dog, is it a he or a she?
98	Michelle:	It's a she.
99	Victor:	How big is she?
100	Michelle:	She's small--about the size of a cat.
101	Victor:	What kind of dog is she?
102	Michelle:	She's a Maltese.
103	Victor:	Who walks her?
104	Michelle:	Mostly my mom, but I walk her sometimes, too.
105	Victor:	Where do you live?
106	Michelle:	I live right across the north entrance of Central Park.
107	Victor:	Is your mom a tiger mom?
108	Michelle:	Not really. She lets me do what I want.

109	Victor:	I wish my mom was like that. All she ever does is tell me to study.
110	Michelle:	Oh, I'm sorry. My mom doesn't tell me what to do, but she doesn't let me play a lot of games.
111	Victor:	How much time do you get to play games?
112	Michelle:	Only 30 minutes a day.
113	Tina:	What's your sister's name?
114	Michelle:	Her name is Rebecca.
115	Tina:	How old is she?
116	Michelle:	She is 11 years old.
117	Tina:	What grade is she in?
118	Michelle:	She is in 5th grade.
119	Tina:	Does she help you with homework?
120	Michelle:	No, not really. She doesn't like to help me.
121	Tina:	What kind of food do you like?
122	Michelle:	I like pizza and spaghetti.
123	Tina:	What city do you live in?
124	Michelle:	I live in Superior.
125	Tina:	Wow, that's quite far.
126	Michelle:	Yea, sort of.
127	Tina:	How long does it take to come to school?
128	Michelle:	It takes about 20 minutes by car.
129	Tina:	Who drives you?
130	Michelle:	My dad drives me in the morning and my mom picks me up after school.
131	Tina:	What do you do in the evening?
132	Michelle:	I do homework and read books.
133	Tina:	What time do you wake up in the morning?
134	Michelle:	I wake up around seven, usually.
135	Mr. Myers:	That is good. We are out of time now. Let's stop here.

Skit 13

TALKING ABOUT WEEKEND ACTIVITIES

2	Ms. Kent:	Good morning, everyone!
3	Kids:	Good morning, Ms. Kent!
4	Ms. Kent:	Good, we will play a Q and A game today.
5	Tim:	Can you tell us about today's topic, Ms. Kent?
6	Ms. Kent:	The topic today will be weekends.
7	Tim:	Are we discussing what we did over the weekend?
8	Ms. Kent:	Exactly. Right on, Tim.
9	Tim:	How should we start the game?
10	Ms. Kent:	Well, start by sharing anything you did over the weekend. For example, places you went, things you did, things you watched on TV, things you ate, and anything else you can think of.
11	Daniel:	We get to ask follow-up questions, right Ms. Kent?
12	Ms. Kent:	Of course. You know the drill very well, Daniel.
13	Tim:	Do you mind if I start?
14	Ms. Kent:	No, not at all. Go ahead, Tim.

15	Tim:	This past Saturday, I biked along the Boulder Creek path with my family.
16	Ms. Kent:	What else did you do, Tim?
17	Tim:	On Sunday, I went to the zoo.
18	Daniel:	Wow, that sounds very interesting. What did you see at the zoo?
19	Tim:	I saw many animals like tigers, elephants, monkeys, and some other ones too.
20	Sam:	Wait, now that I think about it, I was at the zoo on Sunday too!
21	Tim:	Really? What time?
22	Sam:	I think it was in the afternoon.
23	Tim:	Oh I see. No wonder we didn't see each other.
24	Sam:	What about you? What time were you there?
25	Tim:	In the morning at around ten o'clock.
26	Sam:	I see.
27	Daniel:	Isn't that a pretty early start to a Sunday?
28	Tim:	Yeah, but it was okay because we normally wake up around six thirty anyway.
29	Sam:	Wow, that's really early. We don't get up until like 9 o'clock on Sundays.
30	Tim:	Don't you go to church on Sundays?
31	Sam:	No, we don't. We just spend time doing things together as a family.
32	Daniel:	Like what?
33	Sam:	Like shopping, camping, biking, hiking, cleaning, playing games, and visiting friends.
34	Daniel:	I like camping a lot.
35	Tim:	I like biking along the creek.
36	Sam:	I like to bike, too. It's really fun! Especially when you go downhill.

37	Daniel:	Did you go biking this past Sunday?
38	Sam:	No, we ended up going out for lunch because it was my mother's birthday.
39	Tim:	Oh, where did you go eat?
40	Sam:	We went to a Korean restaurant.
41	Daniel:	What did you eat?
42	Sam:	I had bulgogi.
43	Daniel:	How old is your mom?
44	Sam:	I'm not sure. Maybe forty one. She didn't tell us.
45	Daniel:	Who was at lunch?
46	Sam:	It was just our family.
47	Tim:	What did you give your mom?
48	Sam:	I gave her 10 coupons that she can use to have me do the dishes!
49	Tim:	What? Ten coupons to wash the dishes? I don't get it.
50	Sam:	Yeah, ten coupons to wash the dishes.
51	Tim:	How do they work?
52	Sam:	It's simple. Whenever she wants a break from washing dishes, she can use the coupon.
53	Tim:	What happens if she uses a coupon?
54	Sam:	I wash the dishes for her.
55	Daniel:	That's an awesome idea! I'll try that with my mom.
56	Tim:	Oh, I get it now. Wow, I like that idea too.
57	Daniel:	Did your mom like it?
58	Sam:	She absolutely loved it. It surprised her a lot, actually.
59	Tim:	I'm just curious, but how did you make the coupons?

60	Sam:	It's very simple. I just used the notecards you can buy from the store.
61	Tim:	Are notecards the paper slips you use to make flashcards?
62	Sam:	Yea.
63	Tim:	So, what did you write on each one?
64	Sam:	I wrote, "I love you, Mom. Let me help you with the dishes" on each of them.
65	Daniel:	Wow, and then?
66	Sam:	I put them in a pretty envelope and gave them to her.
67	Daniel:	Did your mom say anything?
68	Sam:	Yeah, she said it was the best present she has ever received.
69	Tim:	You know what?
70	Daniel:	What?
71	Tim:	My mom's birthday is next month.
72	Daniel:	Cool. You should use this idea for your mom's birthday present, too!
73	Tim:	Yeah, maybe I'll give her ten coupons to clean the bathrooms.
74	Sam:	I bet your mom will love it.
75	Daniel:	Yeah, that's great but what am I going to do?
76	Tim:	What do you mean?
77	Daniel:	We are going to have a party next weekend for my grandfather's birthday.
78	Tim:	So?
79	Daniel:	I have no idea what to do for his present.
80	Sam:	Oh, well. I'm sure you'll come up with a great idea.
81	Daniel:	I really hope so.

82	Ms. Kent:	Wow, you guys talk very well. I enjoyed listening to you guys.
83	Tim:	We just started talking about what we did last weekend and it led us to all sorts of conversations!
84	Ms. Kent:	Right. That's what I wanted to see. The point is just to start talking.
85	Daniel:	I had a lot of fun today.
86	Sam:	Me too.
87	Ms. Kent:	Good. I am glad to hear that. We are running out of time today. So let's stop here and I'll see you all next time.

SKIT 14

GOING OUT FOR FAMILY DINNER

2	Tim:	Mom!
3	Mom:	Yes, Tim.
4	Tim:	Do we have any ice cream at home?
5	Mom:	There should be some in the freezer.
6	Tim:	Great. Can I have some?
7	Mom:	No, you've been having way too much the past few days.
8	Tim:	The weather is so hot, I can't help it!
9	Mom:	No, no. You have just as much ice cream in the winter too.
10	Tim:	That's because ice cream is so delicious, Mom!
11	Mom:	I know, but too much of anything is never good. Especially sweet things like ice cream.
12	Tim:	Why is that, Mom?
13	Mom:	For one, you can gain a lot of weight from eating too much sugar.
14	Tim:	I haven't gained any weight yet!
15	Mom:	No, you have not. I didn't say you gained weight, but you're not exactly fit either.
16	Tim:	Then, how much ice cream can I have Mom?

17	Mom:	I'd say, maybe once every other day.
18	Tina:	I'm home, Mom!
19	Mom:	Hi, Tina.
20	Tina:	Mom, can I go play with Elvin?
21	Mom:	Where are you going to play?
22	Tina:	Just at the playground.
23	Mom:	Okay, watch out for traffic.
24	Tina:	I will. Don't worry, Mom.
25	Tim:	Mom, can I go biking?
26	Mom:	Sure, just make sure you put on your helmet.
27	Tim:	I will. What time should we be back by?
28	Mom:	We're going out for dinner at five thirty, remember?
29	Tim:	Oh, yeah. I will be back by five then. Is that okay, Mom?
30	Tina:	I will also be back by then.
31	Mom:	Sounds good.
32	Note:	(a couple of hours later)
33	Mom:	(over the phone) Hi, Jim.
34	Dad:	Honey, I am on my way. Are the kids home?
35	Mom:	Yes, Honey. They are playing outside now.
36	Dad:	Oh, okay. Is there anything you want me to pick up on the way?
37	Mom:	Can you pick up the dry cleaning?
38	Dad:	Sure thing. Anything else?
39	Mom:	I think that's it.
40	Dad:	Okay! I need to stop by Grease Monkey for a quick oil change, but I will be home by five ten (5:10)
41	Mom:	Okay, see you then. (hangs up phone)
42	Tim:	(5 pm) Mom, we are home. Is Dad home yet?

43	Mom:	Hi, sweeties. He will be here soon. You guys can go wash first.
44	Tina:	Where are we going for dinner, Mom?
45	Mom:	I don't know. We will see when Dad comes.
46	Note:	(after a little bit)
47	Dad:	Honey, I am home!
48	Mom:	Hi, Jim.
49	Tina:	Hi, Dad!
50	Tim:	Hi, Dad!
51	Dad:	Hey kiddos! How was school today?
52	Kids:	It was good.
53	Dad:	Good. I'm going to go change, but you guys think about what you want for dinner in the meantime, okay?
54	Kids:	Okay.
55	Tina:	Mom! Can we go out for Italian?
56	Tim:	Yea! Can we?
57	Mom:	I don't see why not.
58	Tina:	Yes! I love pasta!!
59	Tim:	I love pizza!
60	Dad:	Are you kids ready to go?
61	Tim:	Yeah, we decided on Italian!
62	Dad:	Okay, that sounds good to me!

UNIT 2

SKIT 1

ASHLEY MEETS BEN

2	Ashley:	Hi, my name is Ashley.
3	Ben:	I'm Ben.
4	Ashley:	Nice to meet you, Ben.
5	Ben:	Nice to meet you, too.
6	Ashley:	Where do you live?
7	Ben:	I live in Westminster. What about you?
8	Ashley:	I live in Westminster, too! What do you like to do for fun?
9	Ben:	I like hanging out with friends and skateboarding.
10	Ashley:	Cool. I like riding go-karts. I also like playing basketball.
11	Ben:	That's cool.
12	Ashley:	Yeah.
13	Ben:	What kind of food do you like?
14	Ashley:	Umm…American or foreign food?
15	Ben:	American?
16	Ashley:	I like pizza, fries, cheeseburgers, and any kind of noodles. Oh! I like steak too!
17	Ben:	Yum. I love steak too!
18	Ashley:	What are your favorite foods?
19	Ben:	I think I like the things you like.

20	Ashley:	McDonald's has really good fries!
21	Ben:	Yes, I know! But it's fast food.
22	Ashley:	It's good though!
23	Ben:	Yes, it is. By the way, who's your best friend?
24	Ashley:	I'm not sure. I have several best friends.
25	Ben:	Just name a few.
26	Ashley:	Okay, this is the girl's list, okay?
27	Ben:	Alright.
28	Ashley:	Rebecca, Courtney, Felicia, and Jennifer.
29	Ben:	The boy's list?
30	Ashley:	Thomas, Daniel, Jacob, and Anthony.
31	Ben:	How do you know them?
32	Ashley:	Some of them are my brother's friends and I know the other ones because of school.
33	Ben:	Cool.
34	Ashley:	Yup.
35	Ben:	Ashley!
36	Ashley:	Yeah?
37	Ben:	Are you free this afternoon?
38	Ashley:	Yes, why?
39	Ben:	Would you like to play tetherball?
40	Ashley:	Sure.
41	Ben:	Let's go play.
42	Ashley:	Okay.
43	Ben:	The winner plays the next person, okay?
44	Ashley:	There is no one else.
45	Ben:	You'll see.
46	Ashley:	(soon after) Wow. Why didn't I see these people before?
47	Ben:	I don't know. Well, let's play!

Skit 2

CHATTY KIDS

2	Note:	Story 1: Waiting for school bus
3	Angela:	Hey Jordan, are you taking the bus today?
4	Jordan:	Yeah, why?
5	Angela:	I'm taking the bus, too! We should sit together.
6	Jordan:	Sure. Where do you live?
7	Angela:	Across the street from the city library.
8	Jordan:	Oh, that's cool.
9	Angela:	Yeah. Victoria is coming with us too, okay?
10	Jordan:	Sure! I don't see why not!
11	Angela:	Here she comes! Oh, and Kyra too.
12	Jordan:	Okay, well, can Erica come too?
13	Angela:	Yeah, we'll be a big group.
14	Victoria:	Hey, guys. Are you all riding the bus?
15	Kyra:	I am.
16	Jordan:	Me too.
17	Erica:	How about you, Angela?
18	Angela:	I'm taking it.
19	Erica:	Well, let's get going!
20	Victoria:	There's the bus!
21	Angela:	What are we waiting for?
22	Jordan:	I don't know! Let's get on!

23	Angela:	Good idea.
24	Note:	Story 2: Ben's uncle and Ruth's aunt
25	Ben:	Guys, guess what?
26	Ruth:	What?
27	Ben:	My dad said that my uncle is visiting from Florida!
28	Ruth:	Is your aunt coming too?
29	Ben:	No, he's still single.
30	Brandon:	How old is he?
31	Ben:	I don't know. Older than 20, I'm guessing.
32	Ruth:	Why are you so excited then?
33	Ben:	Presents!
34	Brandon:	Is he bringing you presents?
35	Ben:	Probably! He sent me a bunch last Christmas.
36	Brandon:	I wish I had an uncle like that.
37	Ruth:	I have an aunt like that. She loves me a lot! She bought me a bunch of presents every year like Santa.
38	Brandon:	Does your uncle buy a bunch of presents, Ruth?
39	Ruth:	No, my aunt isn't married.
40	Brandon:	How old is your aunt, Ruth?
41	Ruth:	I don't know, but I do know she is younger than my mom.
42	Brandon:	Younger than 20?
43	Ruth:	No, but definitely younger than 30.
44	Brandon:	You guys would get a lot more presents if they married each other!

45 Ben: No way! My uncle already has a girlfriend. I've met her before; she's tall and really pretty. She likes me a lot, I think.

46 Ruth: My aunt has a fiance. I heard they're getting married soon. I've seen my aunt's fiance and he is like a football star.

Skit 3

MIRIAM SLEEPS OVER AT CECELIA'S

2	Cecelia:	(At school) Miriam, are you free today?
3	Miriam:	Yeah, why?
4	Cecelia:	Just wondering if you can hang out.
5	Miriam:	Sure! I'll ask my mom to drop me off at your house at...what time?
6	Cecelia:	How about four?
7	Miriam:	Sounds good. I'll be there at four!
8	Cecelia:	Bye!
9	Note:	(4 o'clock)
10	Miriam:	(Knock knock) Hi Cecelia!
11	Cecelia:	Hi!
12	Miriam:	What do you want to do?
13	Cecelia:	Do you want to ding dong ditch?
14	Miriam:	Great! Let's go!
15	Cecelia:	Mom! Miry is here! We'll be back!
16	Cindy:	Ok! Just make sure you're home by five fifteen!
17	Cecelia:	Okay, Mom! We got a new car! A yellow Porsche!
18	Miriam:	Awesome! We're getting a new car, too! A red BMW!

19	Cecelia:	Wow! My favorite car colors are red, yellow, blue, and black.
20	Miriam:	Those are cool colors.
21	Cecelia:	Yeah, they make the car look good.
22	Miriam:	I guess. Sleek looking, you know?
23	Cecelia:	Yeah.
24	Cecelia:	(Doorbell) RUN, Miriam!
25	Miriam:	Come on! Before they see us!
26	Cecelia:	Phew! That was close!
27	Miriam:	Yeah. What time is it?
28	Cecelia:	Five.
29	Miriam:	We have to go back in fifteen minutes.
30	Cecelia:	Call your mom and see if you can sleep over! My mom said you could!
31	Miriam:	Okay.
32	Cecelia:	We have extra toothbrushes!
33	Miriam:	(Miriam calls her mom) Hey Mom! Can I sleep over at Cecelia's?
34	Mary:	I'm okay with it. But, did you ask Cecelia's mom?
35	Miriam:	Yes, her mom said I can.
36	Mary:	Do you want me to bring you a toothbrush and other stuff?
37	Miriam:	No, Cecelia says they have extra toothbrushes.
38	Mary:	Okay, I'll pick you up at eleven tomorrow.
39	Cecelia:	Awesome. Miriam, let's call up some other friends.
40	Miriam:	How about Natalia?
41	Cecelia:	Sure. And Kimberly!
42	Miriam:	Okay. I'll text Natalia, and you text Kimberly.

SKIT 4

PLAYING GROUNDIES

2	Note:	(Situation 1: Calls)
3	Kerri:	So, should I bring some snacks?
4	Ella:	No need to.
5	Kerri:	Okay.
6	Ella:	What time are you coming?
7	Kerri:	Oh, around two.
8	Ella:	Okay.
9	Idaline:	Hey, Ella! (Idaline calls Ella)
10	Ella:	Sup? (What's up?)
11	Idaline:	Nothing much, just getting ready for your party! I'm so excited!
12	Ella:	Same, I can't wait.
13	Idaline:	I wouldn't even be able to talk if I were you!
14	Ella:	Oh, that means I can control my excitement way better than you Idaline. (Jokingly)
15	Idaline:	That's true.
16	Ella:	Just kidding!
17	Idaline:	Yea. Well, it's true.

18	Ella:	Okay, so Kerri is coming around two. When are you coming?
19	Idaline:	I'll just figure something out with Kerri.
20	Ella:	Okay, remember Orlena is coming too.
21	Idaline:	Really? We live so close to each other, we should carpool!
22	Ella:	You do that.
23	Idaline:	Okay. Bye.
24	Ella:	Bye!
25	Idaline:	(Idaline calls Orlena) Hi Orlena!
26	Orlena:	How are you doing?
27	Idaline:	Good, you know about Ella's party, right?
28	Orlena:	Yeah, I know about it.
29	Idaline:	Since we live really close, I was thinking we should carpool with Kerri.
30	Orlena:	Sure!
31	Idaline:	Okay, we'll pick you up, unless you want to come over here.
32	Orlena:	I'll just walk over now.
33	Idaline:	Okay, hurry.
34	Orlena:	I will!
35	Note:	(Situation 2: Going to Ella's party)
36	Kerri:	I can't wait!
37	Orlena:	Same here…
38	Idaline:	You know, Ella is really good at holding in her excitement.
39	Kerri:	Really?
40	Idaline:	Yeah.
41	Orlena:	That's nice to know.
42	Idaline:	I know!
43	Note:	(At Ella's Party)

44	Ella:	Idaline!
45	Idaline:	Yeah?
46	Ella:	You said you would figure something out, and you did!
47	Idaline:	Yes, I did.
48	Kerri:	She knows, like, everything!
49	Idaline:	Actually, I don't.
50	Kerri:	What don't you know?
51	Idaline:	How to hold in my excitement.
52	Ella:	You'll learn.
53	Kerri:	Yeah, you learn that over time.
54	Idaline:	I still don't know how.
55	Orlena:	Okay, okay.
56	Idaline:	Let's go to the park. The park by your house is fun.
57	Kerri:	Let's go!
58	Ella:	Okay.
59	Orlena:	I've never been there.
60	Kerri:	Let's go and see.
61	Orlena:	Okay, then.
62	Note:	(Situation 3: At the park)
63	Kerri:	Do you guys want to play groundies?
64	Orlena:	Sure, but let's get more people.
65	Kerri:	Okay, how about that girl over there?
66	Ella:	I'll go ask her.
67	Idaline:	I love groundies!
68	Kerri:	Me too.
69	Orlena:	Ella, go ask her!
70	Ella:	I'm going!
71	Kerri:	I don't know this park too well, so I have a feeling I'm going to be "it" a lot.

72	Orlena:	I don't know this park well either.
73	Note:	(Situation 4: Ella meeting Dakota)
74	Ella:	Hi, my name is Ella, what's your name?
75	Dakota:	My name is Dakota.
76	Ella:	Cool name!
77	Dakota:	Thanks. Where do you live?
78	Ella:	Right down the street.
79	Dakota:	Don't you like this park? I think it's fun.
80	Ella:	Yeah, I like this park too! It's really fun.
81	Dakota:	Do you have any siblings?
82	Ella:	I have two younger brothers, one older sister, and one younger sister.
83	Dakota:	Cool, I have three younger sisters.
84	Ella:	Wow.
85	Dakota:	Yup!
86	Ella:	What's your favorite color?
87	Dakota:	I like blue. What about you?
88	Ella:	I like purple.
89	Dakota:	Yeah? What's your favorite song?
90	Ella:	Well, I like the Gummy Bear song. It's cool.
91	Dakota:	I've heard of that.
92	Ella:	What's your favorite song?
93	Dakota:	I like Bad Day, the Alvin and the Chipmunks version.
94	Ella:	Cute!
95	Dakota:	What game do you like to play in the park?
96	Ella:	Groundies.
97	Dakota:	Same!
98	Ella:	Great! We, my friends and I, are going to play Groundies right now. Do you want to play?
99	Dakota:	Sure!

100	Ella:	Great, let's go!
101	Dakota:	Thanks!
102	Note:	(Situation 5: Ella's friends are meeting Dakota)
103	Orlena:	Hey, hi!
104	Dakota:	Hi!
105	Ella:	Everyone, this is Dakota.
106	Dakota:	Hi everyone!
107	Ella:	This is Orlena.
108	Dakota:	Nice to meet you.
109	Ella:	This is Idaline and Kerri.
110	Idaline:	Hi Dakota!
111	Kerri:	Hi!
112	Ella:	Let's play Groundies now.
113	Orlena:	Let's get started!
114	Kerri:	I'll be "it" to start!
115	Idaline:	Okay. Thanks.

SKIT 5

GETTING UP, GOING TO SCHOOL AND GOING TO BED

2	Note:	(Situation 1: In the morning)
3	Mom:	Time to get up! Breakfast is ready! Hurry!
4	Note:	(Jacob doesn't answer)
5	Mom:	Jacob!
6	Jacob:	Okay, okay! Coming! Let me wash first, alright?
7	Mom:	Sure, just hurry. The bus will be here in 20 minutes.
8	Note:	(In a moment)
9	Jacob:	What's for breakfast?
10	Mom:	The usual. Bacon and eggs.
11	Jacob:	Mom?
12	Mom:	Hmm?
13	Jacob:	I have a question.
14	Mom:	What is it?
15	Jacob:	Can we go to New Zealand for spring break?
16	Mom:	Jacob! Now is not the best time to discuss spring break plans.
17	Jacob:	Sorry.
18	Mom:	(At the table) Well, are you done?
19	Jacob:	Just about. Okay, I'm done!

20	Mom:	Good, go brush your teeth now.
21	Note:	(In a moment)
22	Jacob:	See you, Mom!
23	Mom:	Bye! Remember to go to your piano lesson after school!
24	Jacob:	Can you pack up my music so that they're ready to go when I get home?
25	Mom:	I can do that.
26	Jacob:	Thanks.
27	Note:	(Situation 2: Night)
28	Mom:	Jacob, go to bed!
29	Jacob:	Okay, let me finish what I'm doing.
30	Mom:	What are you doing, and how long is it going to take?
31	Jacob:	I'm studying for the English test tomorrow, and I'll wrap it up in ten minutes.
32	Mom:	Make sure to keep your promise.
33	Jacob:	I will, don't worry.
34	Mom:	Okay.
35	Jacob:	Actually, can you help me with something?
36	Mom:	Sure, what do you need help with?
37	Jacob:	Can you quiz me on the material?
38	Mom:	Sure. What are you studying?
39	Jacob:	Grammar.
40	Mom:	Oh, never mind then. I was never too good at that.
41	Jacob:	Oh, well.
42	Mom:	Sorry.
43	Jacob:	It's alright. I guess I'll go to sleep now.
44	Mom:	Make sure you brush your teeth.
45	Jacob:	Alright.
46	Mom:	Good boy.
47	Jacob:	Goodnight!

48	Mom:	Goodnight!
49	Note:	(Situation 3: Next morning)
50	Mom:	Jacob, we have a new babysitter.
51	Jacob:	What happened to Michelle? Did she get mad at us?
52	Mom:	No. She's on vacation with her family.
53	Jacob:	What's the new babysitter's name?
54	Mom:	Her name is Rachel. She is 17 and lives up the street.
55	Jacob:	I know Rachel. She gave me a swimming lesson once.
56	Mom:	That's right. And I'm in a book club with her mom.
57	Jacob:	Will she take me swimming?
58	Mom:	Maybe, if you are really nice to her.
59	Jacob:	I hope she gets me a ring pop at the pool.
60	Mom:	I will tell her to get you one, but only if you are good.
61	Jacob:	I promise I'll be good.
62	Note:	(Situation 4: Next night)
63	Mom:	Alright guys, time to sleep.
64	Jacob:	Can we play a little more? Please?
65	Cory	Please?
66	Mom:	No, you can play tomorrow.
67	Jacob:	Oh fine. Come on, Cory. Time to brush our teeth.
68	Mom:	Good.
69	Cory	Mom? Can we play train tomorrow?
70	Mom:	You can talk about that with your brother, okay?
71	Jacob:	Come on, we can play more if we sleep right now.
72	Cory	Okay.
73	Mom:	Now, I want you guys to sleep right away. No hide and seek, understood?
74	Jacob:	Yes, Mom.

JACOB GOES TO THE DOCTOR

2	Note:	Story 1: Visiting Grammy's house
3	Mom:	Jacob. Get ready for Grammy's house.
4	Jacob:	Is Jack coming with us?
5	Mom:	No. He has a birthday party, remember?
6	Jacob:	So it's just me, you and Grammy?
7	Mom:	And your cousin, Molly.
8	Jacob:	Can we play chef? I love to pretend I'm cooking.
9	Mom:	I think that's a great idea. You can make cookies.
10	Jacob:	We need to bring my chef hat and apron.
11	Mom:	I think you outgrew your old apron, but you can use one of mine.
12	Jacob:	What about the one with the flowers on it?
13	Mom:	You can bring that too. But we don't want to be late.
14	Jacob:	I'm hurrying.
15	Note:	Story 2: Visiting a doctor for checkup
16	Mom:	Time to go to the doctor, Jacob.
17	Jacob:	But I'm not sick. Why do I have to go to the doctor?

18	Mom:	You have to get your checkup.
19	Jacob:	Is that when you get a sticker?
20	Mom:	Well yes, but only after a shot.
21	Jacob:	I don't like getting shots. They hurt.
22	Mom:	You don't have to get any this year.
23	Jacob:	So why do I have to go then?
24	Mom:	We need to find out how tall you are and how much you weigh.
25	Jacob:	I think I weigh one million pounds.
26	Mom:	That would be really heavy. I think the floor would break.
27	Jacob:	Okay. 100 pounds then.
28	Dr. Bricker:	(At doctor's office) Okay, Jacob, it is time for your check-up.
29	Jacob:	Do I have to get any shots today?
30	Dr. Bricker:	No, not today. First, let's listen to your heart and lungs.
31	Jacob:	Is this going to hurt?
32	Dr. Bricker:	No, sweetie. It may feel a little cold though. Take 3 deep breaths for me.
33	Jacob:	That was easy. What are you going to check next?
34	Dr. Bricker:	Now I'm going to look at your eyes and in your mouth. Say ahhhhh.
35	Jacob:	Hey, that tickles!
36	Dr. Bricker:	I know. You're doing a great job. Your throat looks great and so do your eyes.
37	Jacob:	Am I all done?
38	Dr. Bricker:	Just about. Here is your sticker.
39	Jacob:	Thanks! That was an easy check-up.

SKIT 7

MOM GIVES RIDE TO RESTAURANT

2	Note:	(Situation 1: Asking for a ride to a restaurant)
3	Imogene:	Mom!
4	Mom:	What is it?
5	Imogene:	Can I go to a restaurant with my friends at six?
6	Mom:	Okay, did you already tell your friends?
7	Imogene:	Not yet. Can Daddy give us a ride?
8	Mom:	Okay, where are you guys going to meet?
9	Imogene:	At our house!
10	Mom:	Okay, I will call Dad.
11	Imogene:	What time is he going to come?
12	Mom:	Well, he usually comes home by 5:30.
13	Imogene:	Okay sounds good. I'll call up my friends.
14	Mom:	Don't you have homework?
15	Imogene:	Nope!
16	Mom:	Are you sure?
17	Imogene:	Yup!
18	Mom:	Why don't you have homework?
19	Imogene:	We had a math test.
20	Mom:	How did you do on it?
21	Imogene:	I don't know!

22	Mom:	We'll have to see, right?
23	Imogene:	Yep!
24	Mom:	What restaurant do you want to go to?
25	Imogene:	Cinzzetti's!
26	Mom:	Sure! The Italian place, right?
27	Imogene:	Yes!
28	Note:	(Situation 2: Dad calls Mom; Imogene calls her friends)
29	Mom:	Hello?
30	Dad:	Honey, it's me.
31	Dad:	I'm calling because I'm going to be late tonight. I have an important meeting with a client.
32	Mom:	Oh my. Imogene is waiting for you.
33	Dad:	For what?
34	Mom:	She is going to a restaurant with her friends, and she is asking for a ride.
35	Dad:	I wish I could, but I'm afraid I can't. What should we do?
36	Mom:	What time can you come?
37	Dad:	Around seven. What's your schedule like this evening?
38	Mom:	I need to prepare dinner.
39	Dad:	Where do they want to go?
40	Mom:	Cinzzetti's.
41	Dad:	Then, why don't you give them a ride to the restaurant, and we will have dinner a little later.
42	Mom:	I see.
43	Imogene:	What time is Dad coming?
44	Mom:	He said he would be a little late because he has a meeting with a client.

45	Imogene:	Oh my gosh! Then, how can we get to the restaurant?
46	Mom:	Don't worry, I will get you guys there.
47	Imogene:	Thanks, Mom.
48	Note:	(Situation 3: After kids get together)
49	Imogene:	Let's hop in my mom's car.
50	Natasha:	Sure.
51	Imogene:	Guys, we're going to Cinzzetti's.
52	Amanda:	I love that place!
53	Imogene:	Good.
54	Natasha:	I've never been there.
55	Amanda:	You'll love it, I'm sure.
56	Natasha:	What kind of food is it?
57	Amanda:	Italian.
58	Natasha:	I love Italian food!
59	Imogene:	We're here, guys!
60	Natasha:	Finally!
61	Natasha:	I'm excited! I can't wait!
62	Imogene:	You won't be disappointed, trust me!

Skit 8

ORDERING PIZZA FOR DINNER

2	Note:	(Situation 1: Talking about kinds of pizza and toppings)
3	Grandma:	What do you guys want for dinner?
4	Mom:	Let's just order some pizza.
5	Grandma:	For dinner?
6	Mathew:	Pizza sounds great!
7	April:	Breadsticks too please!
8	Mom:	Okay.
9	Mathew:	Chicken wings?
10	Mom:	Sure.
11	Mathew:	I saw a coupon for Pizza Hut in the mail.
12	Mom:	We can use that!
13	Mathew:	I like Domino's better.
14	Grandpa:	Well, we have a coupon for Pizza Hut. Let's just use that.
15	Grandma:	We can get Domino's next time, alright, Mathew?
16	Mathew:	Alright.
17	April:	And then Blackjack after that, okay?
18	Brandon:	Yeah, yeah, yeah. Let's just deal with today, shall we?

19	Mathew:	Where's the coupon? I swear I saw it!
20	Brandon:	I have it!
21	Jasmine:	Yum! Can't wait!
22	Dad:	Wow, so how many pizzas do we need?
23	Grandpa:	Let's see, I think the kids could have a pizza to themselves, and the adults could put away a pizza as well, so two.
24	Dad:	That sounds about right.
25	Mom:	So, two pizzas?
26	Mathew:	What kind of pizza should we get?
27	April:	Let's get a pizza with mushroom, sausage, onion, bell pepper, shrimp and one with pineapple.
28	Timothy:	Sounds good to me! Anyone disagree?
29	Mathew:	Pineapple? Gross.
30	Mom:	It's actually pretty good.
31	Mathew:	I tried it once before, and it was not to my taste.
32	April:	Then, you can eat the pizza with all kinds of toppings!
33	Dad:	Kids, can you be quiet? I'm ordering!
34	Pizza Hut:	This is Pizza Hut. How may I help you?
35	Dad:	We would like to order two extra large pizzas.
36	Pizza Hut:	Sure, what would you like on it?
37	Dad:	I believe we agreed on a pizza with mushroom, sausage, onion, bell pepper, and shrimp and a pineapple pizza, please.
38	Pizza Hut:	Alright, anything else for you today?
39	Dad:	Twenty four breadsticks and thirty six chicken wings also, please.

40	Pizza Hut:	Okay, so two large pizzas - one pineapple and one combo with mushroom, sausage, onion, bell pepper, and shrimp? And twenty four breadsticks, and three dozen chicken wings, right?
41	Dad:	That's right! And I have two coupons for five dollars off an extra large pizza.
42	Pizza Hut:	That'll be forty eight sixty four with the coupons. It'll be about 30 minutes. Would you like to pick it up or have it delivered?
43	Dad:	I would like it delivered. My address is 4980 Drew Cir. Unit 123.
44	Pizza Hut:	Got it. Have a nice day.
45	Note:	(Situation 2: 30 minutes later. The doorbell is ringing)
46	April:	The pizzas are here!
47	Brandon:	Mathew, what are you doing?
48	Mathew:	What?
49	Brandon:	Get the door!
50	Mom:	Kids, stop. I will get it.
51	Pizza Hut:	Good evening, ma'am. Two large pizzas, right here.
52	Mom:	(Mom gives fifty two to the delivery person) Thank you. Here you go, keep the change.
53	Pizza Hut:	Thank you very much. Have a good evening.
54	Mom:	Likewise.
55	Grandma:	Now now, kids, have a seat.
56	Tiffany:	Okay, grandma!
57	Brandon:	What kind of pizza is it?
58	Jasmine:	I think this is combo, and that is pineapple.
59	Mom:	That's right, Jasmine!

60	Timothy:	Let's eat!
61	Dad:	Okay, there are twenty four breadsticks total.
62	Mathew:	Well, there are ten of us, so that means roughly we can each get two.
63	Brandon:	That sounds good.
64	Mathew:	I like breadsticks.
65	April:	And there are sixteen slices of pizza, so we each get a slice and a half.
66	Jasmine:	And the same with the chicken?
67	Mom:	No, we get three chicken wings each.
68	Timothy:	Okay. So, two, one and a half, and three.
69	Tiffany:	Yeah, no cheating.
70	Timothy:	What? Why are you looking at me?
71	Mathew:	Yeah, Tiffany!
72	Tiffany:	Whatever.
73	Jasmine:	Hey Mathew! What are you doing to my sister?
74	Brandon:	Yeah!
75	April:	Okay, okay, stop fighting!
76	Timothy:	There they go again! I bet Tiffany wins.
77	Brandon:	Wanna bet?
78	Timothy:	Sure. Ten bucks.
79	April:	Okay, I've got ten.
80	Mathew:	Whatever. Families don't bet.
81	Mom:	Eat the pizza!
82	Dad:	Get eating, kids!
83	Note:	(Situation 3: Talking over pizza)
84	Grandma:	We're going swimming, remember?
85	Tiffany:	Oh yeah!
86	April:	Mmmm, these are good wings!
87	Brandon:	Yes, and the pizza is good too.
88	Jasmine:	I like the breadsticks better.

89	Mom:	I know you do.
90	Timothy:	Dad?
91	Dad:	Yeah?
92	April:	I know what you are going to say, Timothy. Dad can we order from Pizza Hut sometime again?
93	Dad:	I suppose.
94	Jasmine:	Where are we going tomorrow?
95	Mom:	WaterWorld.
96	Mathew:	Really?
97	Mom:	Yeah.
98	Brandon:	I need goggles.
99	Dad:	Yup. We'll go buy them early in the morning,
100	Brandon:	How early?
101	Dad:	Well, all of you need goggles, right?
102	Tiffany:	Right.
103	Mom:	How about if we all go to WaterWorld, I get a stamp for re-entry, go buy the goggles, and come back?
104	Grandma:	Okay. Then we're not wasting time, are we?
105	Grandpa:	Doesn't sound like it.
106	Timothy:	But Mom! You don't know which ones we want!
107	Mom:	Oh, yes I do.
108	Dad:	I'm sure your mom will pick wisely.
109	Jasmine:	I'm sure she will.
110	April:	Okay.
111	Grandpa:	I don't need goggles!
112	Grandma:	Me neither!
113	Mom:	I know that! You're just going to watch anyway.
114	Timothy:	They're lucky.

115	Brandon:	Where are the swimsuits?
116	Mathew:	If they aren't in Mom and Dad's room, they're in the bathroom.
117	Jasmine:	That's what I thought too.
118	Tiffany:	They're there. I saw them yesterday.
119	Mom:	They should be there.
120	Dad:	Why are we talking about this now?
121	Brandon:	Just getting ready.
122	Grandma:	Smart.
123	Grandpa:	Very.
124	Timothy:	I'm going to change into my swim trunks and go. I don't want to change in the locker rooms there.
125	April:	Good point Timothy! I'll do the same, though I will wear my swimsuit, not my swim trunks.
126	Grandma:	It would be funny if you wore swim shorts, April.
127	April:	Yeah.
128	Timothy:	I'm done.
129	Brandon:	Oh, I'm full.
130	Mom:	Let's clean up now.
131	Dad:	Yeah.
132	Tiffany:	Okay.
133	Jasmine:	We're going to WaterWorld, yay!
134	Mathew:	Calm down, Jasmine!
135	Brandon:	I don't think she can.

SKIT 9

ORDERING FOOD AT A RESTAURANT

2   Note: (Situation 1: Ordering food)

3   Waiter: Table for how many?

4   Destiny: Four, please.

5   Waiter: Follow me. Will this table do?

6   Destiny: Fabulous. Sit, guys.

7   Waiter: What would you like to drink?

8   Everyone: Iced tea, Coke, Sprite, Lemonade.

9   Waiter: OK. I will be back in a few minutes to get your orders.

10   Tom: I'll get a gourmet hamburger.

11   Ginger: I'll get a well-done steak.

12   Destiny: And I'll get an extra cheesy lasagna.

13   Tom: Let's all share.

14   Waiter: Here are your drinks. Are you ready to order or would you like a few more minutes?

15   Jake: We'll order now. She's getting a steak, he's getting a gourmet hamburger, she is getting an extra cheesy lasagna, and I am getting spaghetti.

16   Waiter: How would you like your steak?

17   Ginger: Well-done please.

18	Waiter:	Alright. So a well-done steak, a gourmet hamburger, an extra cheesy lasagna and a spaghetti. Is that all?
19	Destiny:	Yes, thank you.
20	Waiter:	It'll be ready in about fifteen minutes.
21	Tom:	Thanks.
22	Note:	(Situation 2: 15 minutes later)
23	Waiter:	Here are your dishes.
24	Tom:	Mmm, they look good!
25	Destiny:	Wow! They sure did make this extra cheesy! Yum, I love cheese.
26	Jake:	Really? Can I have a bite?
27	Destiny:	Sure.
28	Waiter:	Is there anything else I can get you guys?
29	Ginger:	Yeah, could I have some ketchup with my fries?
30	Waiter:	Sure thing. Anything else?
31	Tom:	Oh, some ketchup for me too, please.
32	Waiter:	Two ketchups coming up. Is that everything for you folks?
33	Destiny:	Yes, thank you.
34	Waiter:	Alright. Just let me know if you need anything.
35	Ginger:	Sure will, thanks.
36	Waiter:	Great.
37	Tom:	Whoa, this hamburger is the best hamburger I've ever had! I'm coming to this restaurant more often.
38	Destiny:	This lasagna is kind of plain. Where's the salt?
39	Jake:	Destiny, it's right in front of you.
40	Destiny:	Right. I knew that.
41	Ginger:	Of course you did.
42	Destiny:	I did! How do you like your steak, Ginger?

43	Ginger:	It's good. But it would be better with some pepper.
44	Tom:	Here's the pepper.
45	Ginger:	Thanks.
46	Tom:	No problem.
47	Note:	(Situation 3: after eating)
48	Destiny:	Are you guys done? We should get going…
49	Jake:	I'm not sure about everyone else but I'm full. We should ask for the check.
50	Ginger:	I'm done, too. Excuse me!
51	Waiter:	Is there anything I can get for you guys?
52	Ginger:	Can we get the check, please?
53	Waiter:	Sure. I'll be right back.
54	Note:	(in a moment)
55	Destiny:	How much is it?
56	Ginger:	Thirty five fifty ($35.50). So forty will do it, including tip.
57	Jake:	Sounds about right. We can all pitch in about ten dollars.
58	Tom:	Sounds good. (as he sets down $10) Here is my portion.
59	Jake:	Here is my twenty. Let me take a ten back.
60	Destiny:	Here is twenty for Ginger and myself.
61	Ginger:	(to waiter) Keep the change.
62	Waiter:	Thank you very much.

ELAINE GOES ON A FIELD TRIP

2	Note:	(Situation 1: Evening)
3	Elaine:	Mom, guess what?
4	Mom:	What?
5	Elaine:	Tomorrow, at school, we're going on a field trip.
6	Dad:	Did you give us the permission slip to sign?
7	Elaine:	Yes. And you gave it back.
8	Dad:	So, what's the problem?
9	Elaine:	We're going to a swimming pool.
10	Dad:	I remember that.
11	Elaine:	I need goggles.
12	Mom:	I'm sure you do.
13	Elaine:	It hurts my eyes if I don't have them.
14	Mom:	Oh yes, of course.
15	Dad:	I suppose we can go buy a pair after dinner.
16	Elaine:	Thanks!
17	Note:	(Situation 2: Morning)
18	Elaine:	I like these goggles. I like ones with clear lenses.
19	Mom:	I'm glad you like them, because if you didn't we probably would have to get different ones.

20	Dad:	Good!
21	Elaine:	Thanks, Mom and Dad. Could I ask one more favor and ask for a ride to school?
22	Mom:	I'll give you a ride.
23	Elaine:	Thanks.
24	Mom:	Let's go now.
25	Elaine:	Let me make sure I've got my goggles.
26	Dad:	Yes, you should make sure you've got those.
27	Elaine:	Check!
28	Note:	(Situation 3: At school)
29	Mrs. Kent:	Do you guys have everything?
30	Elaine:	I got new goggles!
31	Mrs. Kent:	Is that so, Elaine?
32	Elaine:	Yes, it is so.
33	Mrs. Kent:	Very nice! Make sure you don't lose them.
34	Madeline:	I have a tie-dye swim suit. How about you, Elaine?
35	Elaine:	I have a pink and white one, striped.
36	Madeline:	Cool, two piece or one?
37	Elaine:	Two.
38	Madeline:	Same here!
39	Elaine:	What a coincidence!
40	Madeline:	Yeah, my tie-dye is yellow and green.
41	Elaine:	I like that color combination.
42	Madeline:	Me too.
43	Elaine:	Ssssh!
44	Madeline:	Why?
45	Elaine:	Teacher!
46	Madeline:	Oh.
47	Mrs. Kent:	Madeline, ssssh.
48	Madeline:	Sorry.

49	Elaine:	Told you!
50	Madeline:	Sorry!
51	Elaine:	Let's have fun!
52	Mrs. Kent:	Does everybody have sunscreen on?
53	Elaine:	Yes, no.
54	Mrs. Kent:	Raise your hand if you don't. I have extra.
55	Elaine:	I need sunscreen!
56	Mrs. Kent:	Okay, come see me.
57	Elaine:	Okay.
58	Mrs. Kent:	Now, close your eyes. I will slather you in sunscreen.
59	Elaine:	Uh oh.
60	Mrs. Kent:	Unless you want to get sunburned. I'm warning you.
61	Elaine:	Whatever, just don't put too much on.
62	Madeline:	I feel bad for you.
63	Elaine:	I'd rather have that done than get sunburned though.
64	Madeline:	Elaine! Come on!
65	Elaine:	What?
66	Madeline:	Let's go!
67	Elaine:	Where?
68	Madeline:	Where the class is going!
69	Mrs. Kent:	Come on, girls!
70	Elaine:	What? Oh, sorry.
71	Mrs. Kent:	Okay, come along.
72	Madeline:	I can't wait!

Skit 11

JAMES STUDIES MATH

2	Note:	(Situation 1: With a Tutor at the School Library)
3	James:	What's up, Daniel?
4	Daniel:	Nothing much. Is there anything up with you?
5	James:	I've got something.
6	Daniel:	What?
7	James:	Homework!
8	Daniel:	Oh, do you not understand something?
9	James:	Yea, I don't get number eighteen (18) in the textbook.
10	Daniel:	Is that the one where you divide three hundred ninety (390) by thirty four (34)?
11	James:	Yeah, that one.
12	Daniel:	So, how many times does thirty four (34) go into thirty nine (39)?
13	James:	Once. I got to that part.
14	Daniel:	Right.
15	James:	And then I subtract thirty four (34) from thirty nine (39).

16	Daniel:	Yes.
17	James:	That's five (5).
18	Daniel:	Right
19	James:	Then you add the zero to five (5), to make it fifty (50).
20	Daniel:	You got it.
21	James:	And then what?
22	Daniel:	How many times does thirty four (34) go into fifty (50)?
23	James:	Once.
24	Daniel:	Right.
25	James:	It says eleven (11) at the top.
26	Daniel:	It should say that.
27	James:	Okay. So fifty (50) minus thirty four (34) equals sixteen (16).
28	Daniel:	Now, you need a decimal on top.
29	James:	Oh! That's what I did wrong!
30	Daniel:	I used to make mistakes like that, too. When I was younger.
31	James:	Thanks for your help, Daniel!
32	Daniel:	You are always welcome.
33	James:	Thanks again for your help! I understand it now.
34	Daniel:	I'm glad. Do you need help with anything else?
35	James:	No, I think I'm okay, thanks.
36	Daniel:	Alright!
37	Note:	(Situation 2: With father at home)
38	James:	Dad?
39	Dad:	Yes?
40	James:	Could you help me with my math homework?

41	Dad:	It depends on what it is.
42	James:	As I said, it's math.
43	Dad:	OK. I can definitely try!
44	James:	Thanks, Dad.
45	Dad:	So, where are you having problems?
46	James:	Well, I got to here.
47	Dad:	Okay. So, what's confusing you?
48	James:	That side goes into the negatives.
49	Dad:	Maybe your previous steps have errors. Let's go through them again.
50	James:	Well, here's the work I did.
51	Dad:	Okay. Let me look it over.
52	James:	Okay.
53	Dad:	Oh, I found the mistake!
54	James:	Where?
55	Dad:	It's a careless mistake.
56	James:	Where?
57	Dad:	See? You're supposed to add those, but you subtracted them instead.
58	James:	Oh! I see!
59	Dad:	Do you think you can do it now?
60	James:	Yeah, thanks, Dad.
61	Dad:	Sure thing.
62	Note:	(Situation 3: With teacher at school)
63	James:	Miss Robin!
64	Miss Robin:	Yes James?
65	James:	I don't get this one.
66	Miss Robin:	How many times have you tried it?
67	James:	Twice.
68	Miss Robin:	Try it three more times.
69	James:	Okay.

70	Miss Robin:	Are you done?
71	James:	Yes, but I'm still confused, especially later on in the problem.
72	Miss Robin:	Let's take a look. Oh, I see the problem.
73	James:	What is it?
74	Miss Robin:	Here, you need to divide by four, not eight.
75	James:	What?
76	Miss Robin:	See here? The one before this one was divided into two parts, so now it's four parts.
77	James:	But the very first one is divided into two parts.
78	Miss Robin:	Yes, because that's the start.
79	James:	Ah! I get it!
80	Miss Robin:	Good! Very good!
81	James:	I think I can ace the test now!
82	Miss Robin:	I sure hope so!
83	James:	Well, that was the only thing I wasn't quite sure how to do.
84	Miss Robin:	I guess you really will ace the test then!
85	Note:	(Situation 4: With mother at home)
86	James:	Mom, I don't get this.
87	Mom:	What subject?
88	James:	Math.
89	Mom:	I'll be right there!
90	James:	Okay, I will work on English in the meantime.
91	Mom:	Go ahead.
92	Note:	(a little later)
93	James:	Mom, when are you coming?
94	Mom:	After I do the dishes!
95	James:	Well, I'm done with my English homework, and don't have any other homework.
96	Mom:	Just wait. I'll be right there.

97	James:	Okay. What's for lunch tomorrow?
98	Mom:	The usual: turkey sandwich and chips, a drink, and a small snack. Do you want something else?
99	James:	No, it's fine.
100	Mom:	I'm coming to help you now.
101	James:	Thanks, I need help with math.
102	Mom:	Math?
103	James:	Yes. I don't get problem number thirteen (13).
104	Mom:	You have to subtract here.
105	James:	Oh! I understand. (solves the problem) Thanks! I'm done with math now.
106	Mom:	Good! Well, go get some sleep now.
107	James:	I will. Goodnight!

SKIT 12

TWO KIDS

2	Note:	Story 1: Sam and James
3	Ms. Kent:	So, what brings you here today?
4	Sam:	James was picking on me.
5	Ms. Kent:	Say what?
6	James:	Was not!
7	Sam:	Was too!
8	Ms. Kent:	Boys! Calm down! What happened? Will one of you explain the situation for me?
9	James:	Well, I called the ball yesterday for today because Sam was playing with it yesterday.
10	Ms. Kent:	Go on.
11	James:	I went outside, and Sam was playing with it again, so I asked if I could have it.
12	Ms. Kent:	Good, I'm glad you talked first.
13	James:	He didn't give it to me, so we just…
14	Sam:	No, that's not true!
15	James:	You were teasing me three years ago in kindergarten!
16	Sam:	That was three years ago!
17	Note:	(Ms. Kent asked a girl to come who was at the scene and the girl comes in)

18	Girl:	I was close to them. From what I heard, it sounded quarrelsome.
19	Ms. Kent:	What did it sound like?
20	Girl:	Oh, just bickering, you know?
21	Ms. Kent:	How did it feel?
22	Girl:	…Tense, I guess.
23	Ms. Kent:	Did you, by any chance, hear fighting?
24	James:	There was no fighting!
25	Girl:	Well, it just sounded like one of them called the ball yesterday but one of them didn't want the other to have the ball.
26	Ms. Kent:	You may go.
27	Girl:	Okay.
28	Note:	Story 2: Steve and Zack
29	Dad:	Okay, guys, go to bed!
30	Steve:	Alright.
31	Zack:	Dad, is it okay if we sleep in the play room downstairs? You know my room is too small for two of us.
32	Dad:	That's fine. Brush your teeth!
33	Zack:	Dad, brushing our teeth is a habit we've had since we were five. We don't need to be reminded.
34	Dad:	Sorry. Now, move along.
35	Zack:	Okay.
36	Note:	(a moment later)
37	Zack:	Alright, as soon as my parents are asleep, do you want to go ride motorcycles?
38	Steve:	Zack, I'm sorry, but I don't think we're old or tall enough.
39	Zack:	It's ok. These aren't real. They're the miniature ones.

40	Steve:	You have those things?
41	Zack:	Two. I got them a month ago.
42	Steve:	Yeah! I'm up for it!
43	Zack:	Great! It's really fun. This will be my third (3rd) time on a midnight ride.
44	Steve:	Really?
45	Zack:	Yeah.
46	Steve:	Thanks so much! By the way, where do we ride it?
47	Zack:	Oh, in front of the house. Thanks to you, too! It's nice to have someone to ride with.
48	Steve:	Aren't they a little loud for night though?
49	Zack:	No. They don't make much noise.
50	Steve:	No way! How?
51	Zack:	They're electric.
52	Steve:	Wow!
53	Note:	Story 3: Jeff and Victor
54	Jeff:	Hey Victor, wake up. Time to go to school!
55	Victor:	Huh?
56	Jeff:	I said, wake up!
57	Victor:	What time is it?
58	Jeff:	Seven forty five (7:45).
59	Victor:	Already?
60	Jeff:	Yeah, why?
61	Victor:	It feels like I just fell asleep.
62	Jeff:	Well, it's time to get up.
63	Victor:	Okay, give me five minutes.
64	Jeff:	Alright. Come downstairs afterwards.
65	Victor:	Where is Mom?
66	Jeff:	She already left for work because of the conference.

67	Victor:	Oh, yeah. I forgot about that.
68	Jeff:	I'm going to go wash now, ok?
69	Victor:	Alright, I'll be down in a few minutes.
70	Jeff:	You'd better be.
71	Victor:	Don't worry. I will be.
72	Note:	(After breakfast)
73	Jeff:	Ready? Did you pack your backpack?
74	Victor:	Hold on. Let me go get my books.
75	Jeff:	I'll be on my way to the bus stop.
76	Victor:	Okay, I'll catch up to you in a little bit.
77	Jeff:	Alright.

Skit 13

AUDREY WORKS ON HOMEWORK

2 Mom: Audrey, how much more time do you need on your project?!

3 Audrey: Hold on. I'm almost done.

4 Mom: You say "hold on" every time I ask.

5 Audrey: (sigh) Do you not want me to do my best?

6 Mom: I want you to do your best, but it's already ten!

7 Audrey: Yeah, but this is a SUMMATIVE grade!

8 Mom: Fine. 20 more minutes.

9 Audrey: I may or may not be able to finish, but I will try.

10 Mom: I'll be reading, so holler when you need something.

11 Audrey: Okay.

12 Edward: You are so slow, Audrey.

13 Audrey: Like you aren't.

14 Edward: I'm going to sleep, holler if you need me.

15 Audrey: You are not going to help.

16 Edward: You know, I can be a lot of help.

17 Mom: What's going on there kids?

18 Edward: Mom, I'm trying to help Audrey, but you know how she is.

19 Mom: Audrey, are you almost done yet?

20	Audrey:	Almost!
21	Edward:	If I help you, you'll be done faster.
22	Audrey:	I don't want your help.
23	Dad:	I'm home!
24	Audrey:	Hi!
25	Edward:	Hi Dad.
26	Mom:	Hello! How was your day?
27	Dad:	Fine! Just fine! What are you guys doing up still?
28	Audrey:	Homework. It's a project.
29	Mom:	It's a big grade.
30	Edward:	And Audrey Allison Thompson won't let me help.
31	Dad:	Edward, don't call your sister by her full name.
32	Audrey:	Yeah, Edward Dylan Thompson.
33	Mom:	That applies to you too, Audrey.
34	Dad:	That's right.
35	Audrey:	Okay. I'm done!
36	Mom:	Go to sleep now.
37	Dad:	You too, Edward.
38	Mom:	Goodnight to both of you.
39	Edward:	Goodnight.
40	Audrey:	Goodnight.
41	Dad:	Have fun!
42	Audrey:	Yeah, yeah. I'll have fun alright.
43	Dad:	Goodnight.

SKIT 14

KIDS GATHER FOR A PARTY

2	Cherilyn:	Mom! Why aren't they coming?
3	Mom:	Cherry, they will be here soon.
4	Cherilyn:	What should I do while I wait?
5	Mom:	Hey, come over here and write their names on these goodie bags.
6	Cherilyn:	Okay.
7	Mom:	How many do we need?
8	Cherilyn:	Well, there is Amber, Faith, Clare, Josephine, Kate, Ginger, Lilia, and Hanna…
9	Mom:	So, one, two, three…eight?
10	Cherilyn:	Just get ten.
11	Mom:	Okay.
12	Cherilyn:	So, what's in them?
13	Mom:	Just goodies.
14	Cherilyn:	Like?
15	Mom:	Small toys.
16	Note:	(doorbell rings)
17	Cherilyn:	They're here!
18	Mom:	Go get the door!
19	Cherilyn:	Hey, guys!

20	Amber:	Hey!
21	Cherilyn:	You guys ready for a blast?
22	Faith:	Are we going to play limbo?
23	Clare:	How about Twister?
24	Amber:	That's boring! Let's play something else.
25	Faith:	Oh, I know what we should play!
26	Clare:	What?
27	Amber:	Hide and seek!
28	Faith:	Or, we can go in the pool!
29	Cherilyn:	How about we go in the pool and get refreshed?
30	Mom:	You guys will need some towels!
31	Cherilyn:	Got them!
32	Clare:	So, who's going first?
33	Faith:	Me.
34	Clare:	I'm second!
35	Amber:	I don't care.
36	Clare:	Is it cold?
37	Faith:	I hope not.
38	Cherilyn:	Nope, it's heated.
39	Amber:	I'm getting in!
40	Faith:	I'm going first, remember?
41	Mom:	I will be back! Have fun!
42	Cherilyn:	I wonder where she's going?
43	Amber:	Whatever!
44	Faith:	Let's party!

Skit 15

CLEANING THE HOUSE

2	Note:	(Situation 1: Getting started cleaning the house)
3	Mom:	Get up, everyone! We're cleaning the house today!
4	Collin:	Do we have to?
5	Mom:	Yes.
6	Nathan:	Fine.
7	Beth:	Let's get started then!
8	Jesse:	Ok.
9	Collin:	It doesn't mean you have to agree on everything just because you're twins!
10	Jesse:	Well, you and Nathan are twins too.
11	Collin:	We are, but we don't agree on everything.
12	Beth:	Well, we do agree on a lot of things.
13	Mom:	Kids, get started!
14	Beth:	Okay, Mom!
15	Mom:	Beth, wipe the dust off the window sills and furniture. Collin, start vacuuming! Jesse, help your sister. Nathan, move the plants outside.
16	Nathan:	Are they heavy?
17	Mom:	Some of them are.
18	Jesse:	Let's go get the dusters.

19	Beth:	Okay, I'll be right there.
20	Collin:	Where's the new vacuum we got yesterday?
21	Dad:	In the closet, first floor.
22	Collin:	I like that vacuum.
23	Dad:	Well, it's new.
24	Collin:	It works well too.
25	Jesse:	So much dust!
26	Beth:	Yeah. My nose is clogged.
27	Collin:	Mom?
28	Mom:	What?
29	Collin:	Where are the filters?
30	Mom:	They should be in one of the closet drawers.
31	Nathan:	Dad!
32	Dad:	Yeah?
33	Nathan:	I need help with this one, it's heavy.
34	Dad:	Okay. Do some of the other ones while you wait for me.
35	Nathan:	Okay.
36	Beth:	Collin!
37	Collin:	Yeah?
38	Beth:	Can we use the vacuum?
39	Collin:	For what?
40	Jesse:	The plants, we need to vacuum the plants.
41	Collin:	Okay.
42	Note:	(with the vacuum)
43	Jesse:	Wow, it goes so much faster!
44	Beth:	And cleaner!
45	Jesse:	Mom would be so happy to see that the plants are so clean! Wow, the money spent on this thing was really worth it!
46	Beth:	I know, and, it saves our energy too!

47	Note:	(Situation 2: Moving plants)
48	Nathan:	Dad! Are you coming?
49	Dad:	Yes, I am.
50	Nathan:	One, two, three, lift! That was hard.
51	Dad:	If you do these a lot, you'll get stronger.
52	Nathan:	Okay. Dad, I need help with this one.
53	Dad:	Okay. One, two, three, heave!
54	Nathan:	That seemed a little easier than the first one.
55	Dad:	Nathan, this one's heavier.
56	Nathan:	Does that mean that I already got stronger?
57	Dad:	Not necessarily. Strength comes with time and effort.
58	Nathan:	I see.
59	Beth:	Collin!
60	Collin:	Yeah?
61	Beth:	Take the vacuum!
62	Collin:	I thought you were using it!
63	Jesse:	Not anymore!
64	Collin:	Okay.
65	Jesse:	The vacuum won't fit through the narrow hall!
66	Collin:	Oh, right…
67	Mom:	Hurry up and get cleaning!
68	Nathan:	Okay, okay!
69	Note:	(Situation 3: Beth slacks around)
70	Beth:	I'm going to sleep, Jesse.
71	Jesse:	Why?
72	Beth:	I'm tired.
73	Jesse:	Okay, but don't blame me if you get in trouble!
74	Beth:	I won't.
75	Mom:	Beth!
76	Beth:	Yeah?

77	Mom:	Where are you?
78	Beth:	In my room.
79	Mom:	Why?
80	Beth:	I'm sleeping!
81	Mom:	Get up and clean!
82	Beth:	What!
83	Mom:	You heard me.
84	Beth:	Fine.
85	Dad:	I think we are almost done with cleaning, guys!
86	Mom:	Then, I will get breakfast ready.
87	Note:	(Situation 4: Breakfast after a while)
88	Mom:	Breakfast, everyone!
89	Kids:	Coming!
90	Dad:	I'm here.
91	Mom:	Guys, we need to finish cleaning after we eat breakfast.
92	Nathan:	What?! I thought Dad said we were almost done!
93	Dad:	You heard Mom.
94	Nathan:	(Mumbling) Fine.
95	Dad:	What's for breakfast?
96	Mom:	Oatmeal.
97	Beth:	Again?
98	Mom:	Yeah, got a problem?
99	Note:	(Collin nudges Beth next to him, and the other kids see that)
100	Jesse:	No, Mom.
101	Beth:	Could we have something else tomorrow though?
102	Collin:	Yes! Please?
103	Mom:	I suppose so.
104	Jesse:	Thanks, Mom.
105	Nathan:	Yeah!

106 Mom: Eat up!

107 Beth: That wasn't so nice!

108 Mom: I know.

109 Collin: Beth, just be quiet for now, will you?

110 Beth: Whatever.

111 Dad: You can talk later, eat now.

112 Jesse: Good point, Dad.

113 Nathan: Hmm, this oatmeal is better than yesterday's!

114 Mom: You sure do love instant food!

115 Nathan: Is that a good thing or a bad thing?

116 Mom: Uhh, let's say it's a bad thing.

117 Beth: Why?

118 Dad: Instant food is bad for your health.

119 Jesse: Yes, but it tastes good.

120 Nathan: I agree.

JOSEPH'S FAMILY TAKES
A TRIP TO FLORIDA

2	Note:	(Situation 1: At school)
3	Joseph:	I can't wait till I go to Florida!
4	Prunella:	You're going to Florida?
5	Joseph:	Yup.
6	Candace:	I'm so jealous!
7	Joseph:	Thanks! I want to go play on the beach.
8	Candace:	I hope you have fun! I'm not going anywhere fancy like that.
9	Prunella:	Neither am I.
10	Joseph:	I'll get you guys souvenirs.
11	Prunella:	Really?
12	Joseph:	Yeah. I mean, Florida is like across the world, so it's special!
13	Prunella:	Yes, but a souvenir?
14	Candace:	Sure, but make sure it's not expensive.
15	Joseph:	Don't worry. That's up to me to decide.
16	Prunella:	When are you leaving?
17	Joseph:	Tomorrow morning.
18	Prunella:	Are you driving or flying?

19	Joseph:	We are flying.
20	Candace:	Well, I envy you. Have a good trip.
21	Joseph:	Thanks. See you when I come back.
22	Note:	(Situation 2: At an airport, Florida)
23	Mom:	Kids, we are finally here in Florida.
24	Joseph:	Wow, I'm actually in Florida!
25	Dad:	The air is different!
26	Jane:	Joseph!
27	Joseph:	Yea?
28	Jane:	We're sleeping in a four star hotel!
29	Joseph:	Really, Mom?
30	Mom:	Yes.
31	Joseph:	Where did this money come from?
32	Mom:	Incentive.
33	Joseph:	You've received an incentive?
34	Mom:	Yes.
35	Jane:	How much?
36	Mom:	Fifteen thousand dollars ($15,000).
37	Jane:	Wow!
38	Joseph:	Really?
39	Mom:	Yes, for the last time this year.
40	Jane:	We're rich!
41	Mom:	We are, but we're going to spend our money WISELY!
42	Jane:	Of course. Let's go shopping every weekend.
43	Mom:	That's not spending it wisely.
44	Jane:	What are you talking about, Mom?
45	Mom:	Going shopping every weekend is not smart.
46	Joseph:	Yeah, Jane.
47	Jane:	But shopping rules the world!
48	Dad:	We have other uses for the money.

49	Jane:	Dad, shopping is wise, is it not?
50	Dad:	If you need something.
51	Jane:	I do!
52	Dad:	What?
53	Jane:	Clothes!
54	Dad:	You've got enough, Jane.
55	Joseph:	Just deal with it, Jane! I know you're addicted to shopping.
56	Jane:	I'm not!
57	Dad:	Kids, stop. Let's pick up a rental car and get out of here.
58	Mom:	Yes. We'd better go check into our hotel.
59	Joseph:	Mom, what about dinner?
60	Mom:	We'll figure something out once we get to the hotel.
61	Note:	(Situation 3: after checking into the hotel)
62	Mom:	Ah, the ocean smells good.
63	Joseph:	Yeah, the ocean color is pretty.
64	Dad:	Let's go walk on the beach. It's a bit early for dinner anyway.
65	Jane:	Ok, I want to play in the beach.
66	Joseph:	Sounds good. Let's go over there.
67	Jane:	Wow, this is the second time I'm seeing the ocean since I was born.
68	Joseph:	Even though it's only spring, it feels like summer here.
69	Jane:	We picked a good place to go for spring break.
70	Joseph:	Mom, Dad, let's go!
71	Jane:	Yeah, let's!
72	Dad:	Honey, what do you think?
73	Mom:	If the kids want to, let's go check it out.

74	Joseph:	Yay!
75	Jane:	Come on! Let's go!
76	Joseph:	I'm going to build a sand castle.
77	Jane:	I'll help you!
78	Dad:	Do you want to make a sand castle we can all live in?
79	Mom:	We might miss dinner then.
80	Joseph:	Let's go make a sand castle all together.
81	Jane:	Yay!
82	Note:	(Situation 4: after building the sand castle)
83	Mom:	It's harder to make a sand castle than it looks.
84	Joseph:	It still looks pretty good.
85	Dad:	It does, doesn't it?
86	Jane:	Let's take a picture of the sand castle we built.
87	Dad:	That's right! High five!
88	Jane:	Yes! High five!
89	Mom:	It's getting dark. Let's start cleaning up.
90	Joseph:	Ok, I'm hungry now anyway.
91	Mom:	Same here.
92	Jane:	What are we going to have for dinner?
93	Dad:	What does Jane want?
94	Jane:	Steak!
95	Mom:	Okay, then let's go back to the hotel and see if we can order a steak.
96	Jane:	Yes!
97	Joseph:	I don't have a problem with steak.
98	Jane:	I think we should take showers before having dinner.
99	Joseph:	Good idea, there's sand everywhere.
100	Jane:	I'm first!
101	Joseph:	Oh, yeah...I forgot about calling things.

102	Jane:	You have to think of these kind of things beforehand.
103	Joseph:	Good for you, since you can do that.
104	Jane:	Well, of course!
105	Mom:	Ok, Jane can shower first and then Joseph will shower second.
106	Jane:	Yay, we're finally here!
107	Joseph:	Hurry!
108	Jane:	I know. I'll be as fast as possible.
109	Mom:	We'd better check if we can order steak from the restaurant.
110	Dad:	Good idea. If we can, we can order it now on the phone so it's ready when we're ready.
111	Jane:	Well, I'd like mine well-done with a lot of pepper then, please.
112	Joseph:	Just go shower.
113	Jane:	Ok.
114	Dad:	Do they have steak?
115	Mom:	(nods) Ok, we'll order now. We'll have four steaks, one well-done with a lot of pepper, one rare, and two mediums. As for salads, we'd like four Caesar salads. And we'll take two vegetable soups, one clam chowder, and one creamy corn. We'll order drinks later.
116	Dad:	You can go shower now. I'll go last.
117	Jane:	Mom, did you order everything?
118	Mom:	Yes. I ordered soup and salad as well. Ok, well, talk to you later. I'm going to shower.
119	Jane:	That was refreshing.
120	Dad:	You look prettier now that you took a shower.
121	Joseph:	Dad, I'm definitely ready to eat dinner now.

122 Dad: Ok, I'm the only one that has to get ready then.

123 Mom: It's your turn now. It is so refreshing that I feel energetic.

124 Dad: Ok, I'm going to quickly shower. Just wait for a little bit.

SKIT 17

MOVIE AFTER SCHOOL

2	Note:	(Situation 1: School gets out)
3	Ms. Kent:	Kids, for homework you will have to read up to page 112 and finish a log.
4	Cliff:	Again?
5	Ms. Kent:	Yes.
6	Lucinda:	Okay. I like this book anyway.
7	Ms. Kent:	Remember Lucinda, you may not read ahead.
8	Lucinda:	I know!
9	Kimberly:	Hey Lucinda!
10	Lucinda:	Yeah?
11	Kimberly:	Do you want to hang out after school?
12	Lucinda:	Sure, I don't have anything after school today anyway.
13	Kimberly:	I was wondering if Ashley could come too.
14	Ashley:	What? Say that again?
15	Kimberly:	Do you want to hang out after school with Lucinda and me?
16	Ashley:	Sure! Can Olivia come too?
17	Lucinda:	I don't see why not.
18	Ashley:	Great!

19	Kimberly:	We can go see a movie.
20	Ashley:	I'd like that.
21	Lucinda:	Tell Olivia, would you Ashley?
22	Ashley:	Okay. (Ashley goes and says to Olivia nearby) Pssst!
23	Olivia:	What?
24	Ashley:	Do you want to hang out after school with Lucinda, Kimberly and me?
25	Olivia:	I think I can.
26	Cliff:	Looks like some girls are hanging out today.
27	Kimberly:	Shush up!
28	Cliff:	Why is it shush instead of shut?
29	Olivia:	That's how we talk.
30	Lucinda:	Yeah.
31	Cliff:	Whatever.
32	Ms. Kent:	What are you guys doing? Write down your homework!
33	Lucinda:	I already did.
34	Ms. Kent:	Good for you, Lucinda!
35	Kimberly:	I wrote mine in my planner.
36	Ms. Kent:	Wonderful.
37	Olivia:	I wrote mine down!
38	Ms. Kent:	Great! Well class is over. Have a great rest of the day!
39	Note:	(Situation 2: After school)
40	Lucinda:	So, what movie are we watching?
41	Olivia:	How about "Nim's Island"?
42	Kimberly:	That sounds good.
43	Ashley:	Sure.
44	Kimberly:	Well, first, we need to check the time.
45	Olivia:	Let's just use the school's computer quickly.

46	Lucinda:	Okay.
47	Kimberly:	I'll go check, you guys stay here.
48	Ashley:	We can all go.
49	Kimberly:	Okay.
50	Kimberly:	There is one at half past three (3:30 pm).
51	Lucinda:	It's three o'clock right now.
52	Olivia:	So, where are we going to see the movie?
53	Ashley:	AMC theaters.
54	Olivia:	Cool.
55	Kimberly:	Let's get walking girls!
56	Lucinda:	Geez, it's hot out here! I can't believe you wanted us to wait for you out here, Kimberly!
57	Kimberly:	Sorry, I just thought it would've been faster if one person went.
58	Olivia:	It would have been faster.
59	Ashley:	Let's just keep walking.
60	Lucinda:	I see the theater!
61	Olivia:	Where?
62	Kimberly:	To your kind of far right.
63	Olivia:	I see it!
64	Ashley:	Me too.
65	Lucinda:	Let's jog.
66	Kimberly:	Okay.
67	Note:	(Situation 3: Purchasing tickets and food)
68	Olivia:	Let's just pay separately.
69	Lucinda:	Okay, that way, there wouldn't be any "You owe me money" thing.
70	Kimberly:	Yeah.
71	Ashley:	Okay, all our tickets are seven dollars.
72	Olivia:	I've got seven.
73	Kimberly:	Me too.

74	Ashley:	Wow, it used to be, like, five dollars, my mom said.
75	Kimberly:	I know.
76	Olivia:	I have my ticket!
77	Lucinda:	Everyone does.
78	Kimberly:	I'll go buy some popcorn. Let's say two larges?
79	Olivia:	Okay. Two of us could share a large.
80	Kimberly:	Okay. I'll be partners with Lucinda.
81	Olivia:	Ashley.
82	Lucinda:	So, Ashley and I can be in the middle.
83	Kimberly:	As you wish.
84	Olivia:	There's a food stand closer to our movie.
85	Kimberly:	Then I'll buy it there.
86	Ashley:	Yup.
87	Kimberly:	Do you want to watch the trailers?
88	Olivia:	Yeah, they're fun.
89	Lucinda:	I usually do.
90	Kimberly:	I do when I'm early. You guys can go in, I'll be in there in a sec.
91	Ashley:	Okay.
92	Kimberly:	Can I have two large popcorns?
93	Gloria:	(Worker) Sure, anything else for you today?
94	Kimberly:	Four small slushies.
95	Gloria:	Okay! Is that it?
96	Kimberly:	Can I have the blue raspberry flavor slush?
97	Gloria:	Sure. Here it is!
98	Kimberly:	Thanks.
99	Gloria:	You need a tray?
100	Kimberly:	I think so.
101	Gloria:	Here, take this.
102	Kimberly:	Thanks.

103	Note:	(Situation 4: Movie)
104	Note:	(Olivia laughs)
105	Kimberly:	My, that seal is funny!
106	Ashley:	This is hilarious!
107	Lucinda:	Look at that pelican thing! Its name is Galileo!
108	Kimberly:	It's cute!
109	Ashley:	I think it's he.
110	Kimberly:	Then, he's cute.
111	Olivia:	Yeah
112	Ashley:	That is so sad! I hope her dad comes back!
113	Kimberly:	I have tears in my eyes.
114	Lucinda:	Kimberly! It's a movie!
115	Kimberly:	I know, but Nim is a really good actress.
116	Ashley:	She is.
117	Olivia:	But Nim is lucky. Her favorite author, Alex Roder came to visit her.
118	Ashley:	She is lucky.
119	Lucinda:	I don't get why she's afraid to go outside though.
120	Kimberly:	Maybe she had a bad experience.
121	Lucinda:	Then, they should show that.
122	Olivia:	Watch the movie, Lucinda! Don't complain!
123	Lucinda:	Okay.
124	Note:	(Situation 5: Going home/at home)
125	Olivia:	My mom called and said that she would pick us up since it's dinner time.
126	Ashley:	Okay.
127	Kimberly:	I'm going to go play in the arcade.
128	Lucinda:	Me too.
129	Olivia:	Guys, she's here.
130	Lucinda:	Okay, never mind then! Wow, she is fast.
131	Olivia:	It depends on the day.

132 Kathy: I'll drive you girls to my house, and you girls can call your moms.

133 Lucinda: Okay.

134 Kathy: Tell them to come here and have dinner with us.

135 Ashley: Yay!

136 Lucinda: We all have a cell phone so…

137 Kathy: Great! You can call now then!

138 Kimberly: Yup.

139 Ashley: Hey Mom!

140 Anna: Yes?

141 Ashley: Kathy said to come have dinner with them.

142 Anna: I'd love to! How was the movie?

143 Ashley: The movie was great.

144 Anna: Did you watch Nim's Island?

145 Ashley: Yes, I think it's my all time favorite so far!

146 Anna: If it was that good, I think I will go see it with Dad.

147 Ashley: You totally should! You will like it.

148 Anna: Alright, thanks, Honey. I'll be there in about 10 minutes.

149 Ashley: Okay. (To Kathy) My mom said she should be here in about 10 minutes.

150 Kathy: Okay. Did all of you girls make a call?

151 Girls: Yeah.

152 Kimberly: So, what's there to do?

153 Olivia: Do you want to go in the tree house?

154 Ashley: You have one?

155 Olivia: Yeah.

156 Lucinda: Sure! I'd love to!

UNIT 3

SKIT 1

GRAMMAR IS DIFFICULT

2 Sunny: Christina?

3 Christina: What now?

4 Sunny: I need help.

5 Christina: With what? (in a careless voice)

6 Sunny: Why are you so grumpy?

7 Christina: Maybe that's just how I am.

8 Sunny: Fine, I'll ask Riley.

9 Riley: Huh? What about me?

10 Sunny: Help me, would you?

11 Riley: I'm busy. Ask Ellie.

12 Ellie: I'm at your service, ma'am (jokingly)!

13 Sunny: How do you do this thing?

14 Ellie: Look, it says "Let's go get some meat vegetables rice chips and some soda." What is wrong with it?

15 Sunny: I don't know! I'm only good at math!

16 Ellie: Do I say "meat vegetables rice chips and some soda" without a break?

17 Sunny: No.

18 Ellie: What puts pauses in sentences?

19   Sunny: A period.

20   Ellie: In a sentence?

21   Sunny: No, I meant, a comma!

22   Ellie: Exactly.

23   Sunny: So it should be, "Let's go get some meat, vegetables, rice, chips, and some soda."?

24   Ellie: Yup!

25   Sunny: Thanks!

26   Riley: It isn't hard, Sunny.

27   Christina: Be quiet.

28   Riley: Yes, ma'am.

SKIT 2

INVITING FRIENDS TO MOM'S PARTY

2	Selena:	(After School) Hi, Faith!
3	Faith:	Hi, Selena!
4	Selena:	Well, I need to ask you some stuff.
5	Faith:	I've got to go soon, but call me, will you?
6	Selena:	I don't know your phone number.
7	Faith:	Oh, it's three nine three, nine eight nine, oh six seven three (393-989-0673).
8	Selena:	Thanks!
9	Faith:	Bye!
10	Selena:	See you later!
11	Faith's mom:	What are you doing in front of the phone?
12	Faith:	Lena is going to call me.
13	Faith's mom:	Who's Lena?
14	Faith:	Selena.
15	Mike:	(Selena at home) Oooh, someone needs to call someone!
16	Selena:	Shush, Mike!
17	Mike:	Why should I care?
18	Selena:	Because you are older and make more calls than me!

19	Mike:	Not this year!
20	Selena:	I don't care!
21	Mike:	Oh yes you do! I see it in your nose.
22	Selena:	Nose?
23	Mike:	Yeah.
24	Selena:	Psssh.
25	Mike:	Psssh. Psssh.
26	Selena:	Okay, so she said three nine three nine eight nine oh six seven three (393 989 0673).
27	Mike:	Who said that?
28	Selena:	Faith.
29	Mike:	Wait, I know someone who has the same number!
30	Selena:	What's his or her name?
31	Mike:	Marcus.
32	Selena:	No wonder. He's Faith's older brother.
33	Mike:	Cool.
34	Selena:	(I am) Going to call her.
35	Mike:	You do that.
36	Selena:	(Calling Faith) Hi, Faith.
37	Faith:	Yo.
38	Selena:	Okay, well on Friday, I'm having a party. Can you come?
39	Faith:	Friday the what?
40	Selena:	The 13th.
41	Faith:	Oooh, that's not good. That's bad luck day.
42	Selena:	Right, so we have a party to get some of the good luck.
43	Faith:	Okay, so your house?
44	Selena:	Yeah.
45	Faith:	I will come by.

46	Selena:	Oh, by the way, my brother knows your phone number.
47	Faith:	What?!
48	Selena:	He knows your phone number!
49	Faith:	How?!
50	Selena:	He somehow knows your brother.
51	Faith:	Oh, okay.
52	Selena:	Good, I thought you were going to have a heart attack.
53	Faith:	I almost did.
54	Selena:	Don't lie.
55	Faith:	Okay, so I will see you on Friday the thirteenth (13th)?
56	Selena:	Yes. Wait, my brother is calling.
57	Faith:	Okay.
58	Selena:	What do you want, Mike?!
59	Mike:	Tell Marcus to come, too.
60	Selena:	Okay! Hello?
61	Faith:	Hi.
62	Selena:	He wants Marcus to come to the party.
63	Faith:	Okay.
64	Selena:	It's a potluck, but you don't have to bring anything .
65	Faith:	Are you sure?
66	Selena:	Yeah, it's actually kind of our mom's party so....
67	Faith:	Oh, okay, so her friends are coming?
68	Selena:	Yep! That's right!
69	Faith:	Okay.
70	Mike:	(Loudly towards the phone) Can Marcus come?

71	Faith:	Hello?
72	Selena:	That was my brother yelling into the phone.
73	Faith:	Oh.
74	Selena:	Well, can he come?
75	Faith:	Let me ask. Marcus!
76	Marcus:	What?!
77	Faith:	Mike is having a party on Friday the 13th, and he wants you to come.
78	Marcus:	I can go.
79	Faith:	Okay.
80	Selena:	Why did you say "Mike is having a party" instead of "Selena is having a party"?
81	Faith:	Because he's more likely to come if I mention your brother's name.
82	Selena:	Good point.

SKIT 3

WORKING ON A PROJECT
WITH FRIENDS

2	Note:	(On the Phone)
3	Charles:	Hey, John! I need some help spreading the word about the fundraiser I'm holding for the tennis walls.
4	John:	Sure. Can my sister Ali come, too? She can help!
5	Charles:	That'd be great. See if you can bring any other kids that can help, including your sister's friends.
6	John:	I will try to get as many people as possible, but how many computers do you have?
7	Charles:	I was thinking of using the school's computer lab.
8	John:	You might need permission from the principal.
9	Charles:	I got it already. See you soon!
10	John:	We're meeting in the downstairs computer lab, right?
11	Charles:	Right.
12	John:	Can't wait!
13	Charles:	Same!
14	Note:	(At School; Computer Lab)

15	Ali:	Hi. Charles?
16	Charles:	Hi, Ali, thanks for coming.
17	Ali:	I heard I need to type something. I was typing at home doing homework, so my fingers should be warmed up!
18	John:	Yeah, she's a fast typist! She types faster than me!
19	Charles:	Well, that's faster than me, because you are faster than me!
20	John:	I don't know about that!
21	Charles:	Did you get anyone?
22	John:	A few, actually. Ali has a couple friends coming, too.
23	Charles:	Where are they?
24	Ali:	I don't know but they're coming!
25	Charles:	Okay. Let's wait for a couple more minutes.
26	Ali:	OK, well they're coming sooner or later.
27	John:	I also got some kids from our neighborhood.
28	Charles:	Who?
29	Ali:	Sierra, Madison, and Miles. They are the only kids that know how to type.
30	Charles:	So your point is they're old enough?
31	John:	Yes.
32	Charles:	How old are they?
33	John:	Miles is eleven, Madison is nine, and Sierra is thirteen.
34	Charles:	I'm fourteen, you are fourteen, and Ali is thirteen.
35	Ali:	Yup, that's right. Here they come!
36	Charles:	Oh, by the way, who are your friends, Ali?
37	Ali:	Oh, are you worried?
38	Charles:	No, I'm not worrying, just wondering.

39	Ali:	Avaleen, and Janet.
40	Charles:	Okay.
41	John:	Alright, this is Madison, and this is Miles, and there is Sierra!
42	Charles:	Hey!
43	Sierra:	What's up?
44	Miles:	Hey!
45	Madison:	Hello!
46	John:	This is Avaleen, and Janet!
47	Charles:	How are you guys doing?
48	Janet:	Great!
49	Avaleen:	Better than great, awesome!
50	Charles:	Madison and Miles seem a little shy. It's alright, we won't bite you!
51	Avaleen:	We sure won't! Sierra and Janet are both outgoing, so just follow their example!
52	Charles:	So, do you guys all know each other?
53	Janet:	Pretty much.
54	Charles:	Great. Let's get going. Do you guys know what we're doing?
55	Madison:	Kind of. John said you would explain when we got here.
56	Charles:	Okay, well this is what we're doing. We are all writing persuasive paragraphs. We're going to plan it all together, though.
57	Janet:	Got it.
58	Charles:	After that, we'll make a list of all the e-mail addresses we know.
59	Avaleen:	I know a bunch.

60	Charles:	Okay, that's good. Then, we will send the persuasive letter to the people on the email list we have respectively. In the email, we are going to mention that we want to make a tennis wall for people to practice tennis without partners and say we need money.
61	Miles:	Hmm. That sounds pretty tough.
62	John:	Don't worry, Miles, we will help each other.
63	Sierra:	We will see how it goes.
64	Avaleen:	Okay.
65	Sierra:	Why don't we make a sample paragraph?
66	Ali:	Yeah. That's a good idea.
67	Sierra:	And then we can just send that to the people on the list.
68	Note:	(Planning Paragraph)
69	Avaleen:	Charles, why don't you start the paragraph?
70	Charles:	Okay. I will write down the information first, and then you guys review it. Okay?
71	Avaleen:	Ok. That sounds great.
72	Sierra:	I play tennis, too. This seems like a great idea!
73	Charles:	Right. And a lot of people just like hitting balls against a wall!
74	Ali:	Yeah, I don't even play tennis. It's just fun to throw balls against a wall.
75	John:	Alright, I think we need to send a letter to the city council and tell them what we are doing.
76	Madison:	I've done this before. I mean, fundraising.
77	Miles:	Great! Then you can give us some tips!
78	Charles:	We need to explain in detail what we're going to do.

79	Ali:	But also, we should get signatures from people who want this to happen.
80	Sierra:	Let's start off by having all of us sign it!
81	Avaleen:	Yeah, that's a great idea.
82	Miles:	I definitely want this.
83	John:	Everyone, let's write the letter first and then create a signature list.
84	Charles:	Yes, that's a good idea, John.
85	Janet:	I know what we should do!
86	Charles:	What?
87	Janet:	I was thinking that we could do the signature thing by e-mail.
88	Ali:	Great idea Janet!
89	John:	We can say, "Do you like playing tennis but don't have a partner? Do you like practicing but can't find a wall?"
90	Madison:	Not bad.
91	Charles:	Sounds decent. We will use that.
92	Miles:	Okay. Charles and John, why don't you make an outline of the letter and a signature form first?
93	Note:	(After outlining the letter and the signature form)
94	Miles:	It looks good to me.
95	John:	Okay. We can pass it around and have everyone edit it.
96	Charles:	Yeah, when you get it, you can write a suggestion on it.
97	Avaleen:	We should put a deadline on replying or submitting signatures.
98	Madison:	Yes. We need a deadline.

99	Ali:	It should be a short period. If it's too long, people might forget about it.
100	Sierra:	True.
101	Avaleen:	What about two weeks from now?
102	Charles:	Okay. Two weeks from now. That will be April tenth.
103	Sierra:	Sounds good. Charles, please send the final email outline to us first. Then we will send it to our own email list respectively. How's that?
104	Miles:	Oh, I need to check my email list. Maybe I can find some more.
105	John:	Also, if we can get the city council email list, that would be great.
106	Ali:	I think you can find the list if you check the city's website.
107	Miles:	That's a good idea!
108	Sierra:	I'll take the extra list like the city council or the Better Business Bureau.
109	Madison:	Good luck, Sierra.
110	John:	Someday, we should go to a busy place and get some signatures too.
111	Madison:	Later, maybe. Okay. Let's start!
112	Charles:	Everybody, let's get started and thank you so much for your help!

SKIT 4

BIRTHDAY PARTY

2	Note:	(Birthday party planning)
3	Lola:	So, your birthday party is a sleepover?
4	Pam:	Yeah, bring your sleeping bag.
5	Lola:	Okay. Who else is coming?
6	Pam:	I'm not telling! It's a surprise!
7	Lola:	I understand.
8	Pam:	I just wanted to make this party a surprise one.
9	Lola:	Sure, sounds great.
10	Note:	(Party)
11	Lola:	Where is everyone, Pam?
12	Pam:	They're not here yet.
13	Lola:	Cool. I like being the first one!
14	Pam:	I like being first, too!
15	Note:	(Doorbell Rings)
16	Pam:	Here they are!
17	Lola:	They? I only see Tina.
18	Pam:	Well, here is Tina!
19	Tina:	Hi!
20	Pam:	Actually, Lola and you are the only ones.
21	Tina:	Nice!

22	Lola:	So that's how you kept it a secret!
23	Pam:	Yep. I only wanted to invite a few people so that they could keep it to themselves.
24	Tina:	I wouldn't have thought of that.
25	Pam:	Well, let's get going on the activities!
26	Tina:	They must be simple ones since there are only three of us.
27	Pam:	They're simple, but fun.
28	Note:	(Activities)
29	Lola:	So, what are we going to do?
30	Pam:	Well, I was thinking we can do the piñata first, and have the candy while we party.
31	Lola:	Sounds great.
32	Pam:	Okay. How about Tina goes first, then me, then Lola?
33	Tina:	Are you sure you don't want to go first, Pam?
34	Pam:	No, no, it's fine!
35	Tina:	Alright, well here I go!
36	Pam:	Close. My turn. Ready, hit!
37	Lola:	I think after my turn, it'll open.
38	Tina:	You're right! It opened!
39	Pam:	Let's pick up the candy.
40	Lola:	Oooh! There are Nerds! I love Nerds!
41	Tina:	And Laffy Taffy! I like Laffy Taffy better than Nerds.
42	Pam:	Well, I like Sweettarts and Nerds.
43	Tina:	I can't believe that you guys don't like Laffy Taffy.
44	Lola:	I don't know why I don't like it, I just don't.
45	Pam:	It's too sticky.
46	Tina:	Why did you buy it then?

47	Pam:	Oh, they were all in a pack together. Now, we're going to see who's the best at using chopsticks!
48	Lola:	How are we going to do that?
49	Pam:	We have a bowl of jellybeans and with chopsticks, we are going to see who can get the most jellybeans into the other bowl.
50	Lola:	Fun.
51	Pam:	You can do it anyway you want, but no matter what, you can't use your hands!
52	Tina:	What are we going to do with the jellybeans?
53	Pam:	The ones you get, you can eat!
54	Lola:	Cool!
55	Note:	(At Night)
56	Lola:	Let's stay up until midnight!
57	Tina:	Let's do it! If we had more people, we could have a slumber party.
58	Pam:	Okay, whoever goes to sleep first will be the victim.
59	Tina:	What if you fall asleep first? We don't know what to do!
60	Pam:	If I do, though I doubt it, wake me up.
61	Lola:	What if you don't wake up?
62	Pam:	Don't worry, I'm a very light sleeper.
63	Tina:	Okay. You'd better be.
64	Pam:	I am, even my family thinks so.
65	Lola:	I'm relieved.
66	Note:	(a little bit later)
67	Pam:	Lola! I think Tina's asleep!
68	Lola:	I think so too.
69	Pam:	I'll go get some whipped cream. Stay here.
70	Lola:	Okay, but what are we going to do with it?

71	Pam:	Put it in Tina's hand, and tickle her nose with a Q-tip.
72	Lola:	What will that do?
73	Pam:	It'll make her sneeze, and she'll put her hand with whipped cream in it to her mouth!
74	Lola:	Oh gosh, that's going to be funny.
75	Pam:	Let me go get the whipped cream.
76	Lola:	This is like the best party ever!
77	Pam:	Shh ~
78	Lola:	Is the whipped cream in a can or container?
79	Pam:	Can.
80	Lola:	I like the taste of the canned one better.
81	Pam:	It's sweet. Lola, will you put some in her right hand?
82	Lola:	Why does it matter?
83	Pam:	Well, I know that Tina sleeps early, so I was watching her to see if she covered her mouth with her right hand or her left hand when she sneezes.
84	Lola:	I didn't notice that you were studying her!
85	Pam:	Well, I kind of wasn't.
86	Lola:	Okay. So her right hand.
87	Pam:	Yup. I will go get a Q-tip.
88	Lola:	Okay.
89	Pam:	Lola, when she wakes up, pretend to sleep.
90	Lola:	Okay.
91	Pam:	Tickle, tickle, tickle!
92	Lola:	Shush!
93	Pam:	Pretend to sleep now!
94	Tina:	Achoo! What is this?!

95	Pam:	(in a tired voice) What are you talking about, Tina?
96	Tina:	There's whipped cream in my hand!
97	Lola:	What?
98	Tina:	I sneezed, and there was whipped cream in my hand!
99	Pam:	Sorry, we did that. Hahaha
100	Tina:	Ah, so I was the victim.
101	Note:	(morning)
102	Pam:	I'm hungry. Let's have some pancakes for breakfast.
103	Tina:	Sure. I can still feel some whipped cream on my hands.
104	Lola:	It was funny last night.
105	Pam:	Yeah, really funny.
106	Tina:	So, you guys did put the whipped cream on my hand.
107	Lola:	Sorry, but it was fun. Anyway, the pancakes are almost ready!
108	Tina:	I'll take revenge on you next time.
109	Lola:	As you wish… Let's have pancakes now.
110	Pam:	Wait a minute. I need to flip this pancake.
111	Lola:	Can I help?
112	Tina:	I'm not good at flipping pancakes.
113	Pam:	I can do it.
114	Lola:	I want to do it, too!
115	Pam	I'll do this, you do the next one.

SKIT 5

BUYING A PHONE

2	Amy:	Dad, can I get a phone?
3	Dad:	I think you can. I'll have to talk to your Mom, though.
4	Amy:	Come on!
5	Megan:	Can I get one, too?
6	Dad:	No, you are too young. Amy is twelve, and you are only four!
7	Megan:	Fine, but can I get one when I turn twelve?
8	Dad:	Of course.
9	Megan:	How about Lillian?
10	Dad:	When she is twelve. You don't need to worry!
11	Note:	(Mom comes home)
12	Amy:	Dad! Mom's home!
13	Dad:	Why are you so elated?
14	Amy:	You know why!
15	Dad:	Right. Beth, Amy wants a phone. I said okay. What do you say?
16	Mom:	I don't know about that. Umm… I think it will be okay as long as Dad agrees.
17	Amy:	Thanks, Mom.
18	Mom:	Okay, Honey.

19	Megan:	Can I choose the phone, Amy?
20	Amy:	Maybe, little sister.
21	Megan:	I don't like being called little sister! Call me Megan, or sister, or sis.
22	Amy:	Okay, sorry.
23	Megan:	Good.
24	Amy:	There's nothing wrong with being called little sister! Lillian is even smaller than you.
25	Megan:	Then call Lillian little sister.
26	Amy:	If you wish.
27	Note:	(The next day)
28	Amy:	Dad! Can we go get my phone today?
29	Megan:	I'm going, too! Amy said she might let me choose her phone.
30	Amy:	I said maybe!
31	Dad:	After breakfast!
32	Amy:	Alright, alright.
33	Note:	(After breakfast)
34	Megan:	Let's go! Amy, will you let me play with your phone?
35	Amy:	Sure.
36	Dad:	Ready?
37	Amy:	Yes! I can't wait!
38	Dad:	What do you think you're going to get?
39	Amy:	What do you mean?
40	Dad:	What type of phone?
41	Amy:	I don't know. I was thinking about a Venus.
42	Note:	(At the phone dealer shop)
43	Worker:	How may I help you today?
44	Dad:	We would like to get a phone. Is it possible to get a discount since we are adding another line?

45	Worker:	There is no discount, but there is something called a family plan. You can switch to the family plan anytime. For example, the whole family gets to share two thousand minutes per month.
46	Dad:	Sounds great!
47	Worker:	So would you like to start a family plan today?
48	Dad:	Sure!
49	Worker:	So what are the numbers you already have?
50	Dad:	Mine is seven two zero, three two one, five five seven seven (720 321 5577). My wife's number is seven two zero, nine eight seven, six five four three (720 987 6543).
51	Worker:	Cool numbers!
52	Dad:	Yes.
53	Worker:	So you would like to add a line to the family plan today?
54	Dad:	Yes, please.
55	Worker:	Adding a line is ten dollars.
56	Dad:	Alright, that's fine!
57	Worker:	It's all set!
58	Dad:	Great. Does she get to choose her phone now?
59	Worker:	Of course! What kind of phone would you like, miss?
60	Amy:	A pink Venus.
61	Worker:	Of course. Here it is! You're all set to go!
62	Dad:	Thank you. Ready to go, girls?
63	Megan:	I didn't get to choose the phone!
64	Amy:	You'll like this one, I know it.
65	Megan:	Okay.
66	Dad:	Thanks!
67	Worker:	Anytime!

68	Amy:	Finally, I have a phone!
69	Dad:	I know you've been waiting for it, and you deserve it.
70	Megan:	Will I deserve one when I'm twelve?
71	Dad:	We'll have to see about that!
72	Note:	(At home)
73	Mom:	Let me see what you got, Amy!
74	Amy:	I got a pink Venus!
75	Mom:	Wow, very nice. Cool, I like it.
76	Megan:	Amy said that I'll like the pink Benus.
77	Amy:	Benus? What are you talking about?
78	Megan:	Your pink Benus!
79	Amy:	Oh, my pink Venus!
80	Megan:	Right, Benus.
81	Amy:	Say Venus.
82	Megan:	Venus.
83	Amy:	There we go.
84	Lillian:	(gibberish) Goo a poo la hoo.
85	Amy:	What is she saying?
86	Mom:	I think Lillian wants to see your phone.
87	Amy:	Hi, Lillian. You want to see my phone?
88	Lillian:	(gibberish) Macoo ga.
89	Amy:	Okay, then. Here it is! No, don't touch it.
90	Mom:	I wouldn't let her touch it if I were you.
91	Megan:	Me neither. Lillian has spit all over her face! That's gross.
92	Dad:	That's enough about Lillian.
93	Amy:	Dad, when is it going to be activated?
94	Dad:	It should be activated soon. Maybe in a day or two.
95	Megan:	Why isn't it already activated?

96	Dad:	Oh, the manager set it that way.
97	Megan:	Cool.
98	Mom:	Let me see your phone again, Amy.
99	Amy:	It's so cool!
100	Dad:	I wasn't that excited when I got my phone!
101	Megan:	You should have been.
102	Dad:	Well, I wasn't.
103	Megan:	Why?
104	Dad:	Because Dad was an adult.
105	Lillian:	(gibberish) Bahbgoo.
106	Megan:	I'm tired.
107	Mom:	It's nap time.
108	Amy:	I'll take her to bed.
109	Dad:	Thanks, Amy.
110	Megan:	Sleep with Amy?
111	Mom:	Yeah. Go ahead.
112	Amy:	Let's go, Megan.
113	Megan:	Ok.
114	Amy:	You need to brush your teeth first.
115	Megan:	Ok.
116	Amy:	What a good girl, Megan!

SKIT 6

MAKING PHONE CALLS TO FRIENDS

2	Note:	(Lucas returning Mark's call)
3	Mary:	Hello?
4	Lucas:	Hi, could I talk to Mark please?
5	Mary:	Who is this?
6	Lucas:	This is Lucas. I'm returning his call.
7	Mary:	Hi, Lucas. How are you?
8	Lucas:	Fine. Thank you.
9	Mary:	Hold on a minute. I will get Mark for you.
10	Lucas:	Thank you.
11	Mary:	You are welcome. Mark! Phone call for you. Get the phone, it's Lucas.
12	Mary:	Hey, Lucas.
13	Lucas:	Yes?
14	Mary:	I thought Mark was upstairs but it seems like he's outside walking his dog. Can I have him call you when he comes back?
15	Lucas:	Sure.
16	Mary:	What's your number?
17	Lucas:	He has my number but just in case, it's three oh three, four six six, six eight six nine (303-466-6869).

18	Mary:	Okay, I will let him know that you called.
19	Lucas:	Thank you.
20	Mary:	You're welcome.
21	Lucas:	Bye.
22	Mary:	Bye.
23	Note:	(After Mark comes back)
24	Mary:	Where have you been, Honey?
25	Mark:	I was walking the dog around the park.
26	Mary:	I thought so. Lucas called you.
27	Mark:	When?
28	Mary:	Well, it's been about 30 minutes.
29	Mark:	Oh, thanks, Mom.
30	Mary:	You are welcome. You know his number?
31	Mark:	Yeah, I have him in my contacts.
32	Mary:	Okay.
33	Note:	(Mark calling Lucas)
34	Mark:	Hi, Lucas, this is Mark.
35	Lucas:	Oh, hi!
36	Mark:	So, what are you up to?
37	Lucas:	Not much. Just a little bit of summer reading to do, but that's all.
38	Mark:	Cool. I was going to ask if you were up to playing some tennis before break ends.
39	Lucas:	That would be nice.
40	Mark:	When are you available?
41	Lucas:	I'm free Mondays through Saturdays but on Sundays I have to go to church.
42	Mark:	Well, I can do it anytime.
43	Lucas:	Okay. Let's meet at the Broomfield Community Center tennis courts on Thursday. Would that work for you?

44	Mark:	Sure. Make sure to bring your racquet, water, sunscreen, tennis balls, hat, good shoes -
45	Lucas:	(cuts Mark off) Okay! I got it.
46	Mark:	Well, I'll see you on Thursday then. Wait, what time?
47	Lucas:	Let's make it from 7:00 O'clock AM to 11:00 O'clock AM.
48	Mark:	Got it.
49	Note:	(Evening phone call after playing tennis on Thursday)
50	Mark:	Hello?
51	Lucas:	Hey, Mark. How was tennis today?
52	Mark:	Great. Just a little tiring.
53	Lucas:	Yeah, same here. It was fun though. We should do that again sometime.
54	Mark:	Definitely. Oh, by the way, my mom told me that she will get me a new racquet.
55	Lucas:	Really? You are so lucky.
56	Mark:	You are too.
57	Lucas:	Why?
58	Mark:	Because we're getting you one, too!
59	Note:	(Lucas is silent)
60	Mark:	Hello?
61	Lucas:	Yeah?
62	Mark:	What's wrong?
63	Lucas:	Nothing. Hey, Mark, are you for real?
64	Mark:	Yeah. I talked to my mom about it and she said yes. I think she's spoiling me.
65	Lucas:	Well, thanks.
66	Mark:	Sure thing. You want to go get it tomorrow?
67	Lucas:	Does that work for you?

68	Mark:	Yeah. Does it work for you?
69	Lucas:	Yeah.
70	Mark:	You might want to do some research online though.
71	Lucas:	Why?
72	Mark:	Because there are many types. You want to find one that fits you.
73	Lucas:	Thanks, man. I don't know how to pay you back.
74	Mark:	Don't worry about it.
75	Lucas:	Well, thanks again.
76	Mark:	You are welcome. See you tomorrow then.
77	Lucas:	Okay, bye.
78	Mark:	Bye.
79	Note:	(The next day)
80	Mary:	How are you, Lucas?
81	Lucas:	I'm fine. How are you?
82	Mary:	Great.
83	Lucas:	Thank you so much for getting me a racquet.
84	Mary:	No problem. Mark wanted a Babolat. What about you? Do you have anything in mind?
85	Lucas:	I'm leaning towards a Babolat as well.
86	Mary:	Cool. Hop on. Let's go.
87	Note:	(at the store)
88	Mary:	Could we please purchase a Babolat Aero Storm and Pure Drive?
89	Sam	Sure. Do you have any string preferences?
90	Mary:	No. Anything is fine.
91	Sam	Alright. I'll have it done within two hours. You can pick them up then.
92	Mary:	Thank you.
93	Note:	(After Mark and Lucas get their racquets)

94	Mary:	Hey, do you guys want to try out your new racquets?
95	Mark:	Sure! Could you drop us off at the courts?
96	Mary:	Of course. Does that work for you, Lucas?
97	Lucas:	Yes, but I have to be home by seven because we're having some people over. You guys should come!
98	Mary:	Really? Thanks! That works for me but is that okay with your parents?
99	Lucas:	Yeah I'm pretty sure that they'll be fine with it.
100	Mary:	Well, you should call your mom to check. I don't want to show up unexpectedly and intrude on anything.
101	Lucas:	Okay. I'll call her in a minute then call you back.
102	Mary:	Sounds great.
103	Note:	(After playing tennis)
104	Mark:	Wow! I really like this racquet.
105	Lucas:	Same! I should call my mom now.
106	Mark:	Yeah.
107	Note:	(The phone call of Lucas and his mom)
108	Lucy:	Hello?
109	Lucas:	Mom?
110	Lucy:	Yeah, what's up? You know, you have to be home by seven, right?
111	Lucas:	Yes, I know. I wanted to ask if Mark and his mom could come over.
112	Lucy:	Sure, why not!
113	Lucas:	Awesome. Yeah, Mary just bought me a new racquet.
114	Lucy:	No way! Wow, that's a lot.
115	Lucas:	Yeah, I know. I just wanted to pay them back somehow, and I thought this was a good opportunity.

116	Lucy:	Well, do as you wish.
117	Lucas:	Awesome. See you soon.
118	Lucy:	Alright. Bye.
119	Mark:	What did she say?
120	Lucas:	She said you guys are welcome to come over.
121	Mark:	Cool. Could I use your phone to call my mom? I left mine at home.
122	Lucas:	Sure. Here you go.
123	Note:	(Mark's phone call)
124	Mary:	This is Mary.
125	Mark:	Mom, Lucas's mom said…
126	Mary:	Hurry up. I'm driving right now.
127	Mark:	Okay. She said yes, we can come over.
128	Mary:	Wonderful. I'll pick you guys up right now, since it's twenty till. We can stop by at our house, so you can take a fast shower or something.
129	Mark:	Okay, then. See you soon.
130	Mary:	Bye.
131	Mark:	Bye.

SKIT 7

RAISING A DOG

2	Jacob:	Mom!
3	Mom:	Yes?
4	Jacob:	You said I can get a dog, right?
5	Mom:	Right.
6	Calvin:	You did say that, Mom?
7	Jacob:	Well, I found a lab and a German Shepherd mix online.
8	Mom:	Did you now?
9	Jacob:	He's one month old, and very cute.
10	Mom:	How much?
11	Calvin:	Geez Mom, why do you always ask the price first?
12	Mom:	All the information is useless if the price is out of our range!
13	Jacob:	Okay, it's two hundred.
14	Mom:	Why so expensive?
15	Calvin:	All dogs are like that, Mom.
16	Mom:	Really? Go get Vivian.
17	Calvin:	Okay.
18	Jacob:	No!
19	Mom:	Why not?
20	Jacob:	She won't agree!

21	Calvin:	Jacob, she needs to agree.
22	Jacob:	Fine.
23	Calvin:	Vivian!
24	Vivian:	Yeah?
25	Calvin:	Come over here!
26	Vivian:	Why?
27	Jacob:	We're choosing our dog!
28	Vivian:	I'll be right there.
29	Mom:	Hurry, Vivian!
30	Vivian:	Okay! I'm coming.
31	Jacob:	How's this dog?
32	Vivian:	Sure! He's cute!
33	Calvin:	You got to be kidding me, Vivian!
34	Vivian:	I'm not!
35	Jacob:	How did you know it's a boy?
36	Vivian:	I don't know. I just know if it's a boy or a girl.
37	Jacob:	Okay, I want to try something with Vivian.
38	Vivian:	Fine with me!
39	Calvin:	What gender is this dog?
40	Vivian:	Boy.
41	Calvin:	Wow. That was right!
42	Vivian:	Try another dog.
43	Jacob:	How about this one?
44	Vivian:	Boy.
45	Jacob:	Whoa.
46	Vivian:	One more!
47	Calvin:	This one.
48	Vivian:	Girl.
49	Jacob:	Mom, Vivian has a weird talent!
50	Mom:	Yes, she does!
51	Vivian:	Well, are we getting this dog?

52	Mom:	Yes, if you guys want it.
53	Jacob:	Thanks, Mom!
54	Calvin:	Buy him now, Jacob!
55	Jacob:	Where do I pay?
56	Mom:	Right there!
57	Jacob:	Oh! I didn't see that. Sorry.
58	Mom:	Do you need my credit card?
59	Jacob:	Yeah.
60	Mom:	Here you go.
61	Calvin:	When will he arrive?
62	Vivian:	Yeah, when?
63	Jacob:	We have to go pick him up in a week.
64	Calvin:	One week?
65	Jacob:	Yes. The owner is out of town until next week.
66	Calvin:	I want a closer look at him.
67	Vivian:	Me too.
68	Jacob:	Just don't change your mind, okay?
69	Calvin:	I won't. Don't worry.
70	Vivian:	I don't know about that.
71	Jacob:	Let's just hope.
72	Vivian:	I like him alright!
73	Mom:	I like him, too.
74	Vivian:	How about Dad?
75	Mom:	He agreed to let you guys choose.
76	Calvin:	Awesome!
77	Mom:	Remember, your dad will be home in nine (9) days from his business trip!
78	Vivian:	So, we'll nurture the puppy, and show Dad when he comes!
79	Jacob:	Right!
80	Calvin:	Perfect timing!

81	Vivian:	(Next day, talking to Kim, a friend) Guess what happened last night!
82	Kim:	What happened? Why are you so jumpy?
83	Vivian:	I got a new puppy. It's really cute.
84	Kim:	What kind is it?
85	Vivian:	It's a mutt. A mutt is like a poodle, right?
86	Kim:	A mutt just means that it is not a purebred.
87	Vivian:	What's a purebred? Like the bread we eat?
88	Kim:	No, silly. It means that both the mom and dad are the same kind of dog.
89	Vivian:	Like both poodles?
90	Kim:	Yeah. What kind of dogs are the mom and dad?
91	Vivian:	I think one is a German Shepherd and the other is a Labradeer.
92	Kim:	A Labrador?
93	Vivian:	That's right. And it's brown.
94	Note:	(Couple of days after bringing the dog home)
95	Vivian:	Calvin! Where did you put the leash from last time?
96	Calvin:	I don't know! Why are you asking me?
97	Vivian:	Because you walked Ralphy last time!
98	Calvin:	It should be where it normally is.
99	Vivian:	Well, it isn't!
100	Calvin:	Look more carefully!
101	Vivian:	I did! It's not there.
102	Calvin:	Ask Jacob.
103	Vivian:	Jacob!
104	Jacob:	What?
105	Vivian:	Where is Ralphy's leash?
106	Jacob:	I hid it.
107	Calvin:	Why?

108	Jacob:	I want Ralphy to know not to run away.
109	Vivian:	I don't know if this is a good idea.
110	Jacob:	I hope he's a quick learner.
111	Calvin:	I really hope you're right, Jacob.
112	Jacob:	Go Vivian!
113	Vivian:	I'm going, Jacob.
114	Calvin:	Oh, great. I'll go with you, in case Ralphy runs away.
115	Vivian:	Here we go! Come on, Ralphy, you're staying with me since you don't have a leash.
116	Ralphy:	Woof woof! (barking)
117	Vivian:	Ralphy, do you want to walk on the ground? Okay, here (lets Ralphy down).
118	Calvin:	I think Ralphy likes it on the ground better.
119	Vivian:	Why does Jacob have to think like that?
120	Calvin:	Well, it'd be nice if Ralphy knew not to run away. I guess I understand him.
121	Vivian:	I guess so.
122	Calvin:	No! No, bad boy, Ralphy!
123	Ralphy:	Grrrrrrr. Roof!
124	Vivian:	Don't let him see the other dogs.
125	Calvin:	Let's just hope he doesn't.
126	Vivian:	It would have been nice if Jacob gave us the leash!
127	Calvin:	Yeah, but if he had given it to us, Ralphy would already be on the leash.
128	Vivian:	True. It's riskier this way, though.
129	Ralphy:	Grrrr. Woof! (growling, barking)
130	Calvin:	Fun.
131	Note:	(Ralphy escapes)
132	Vivian:	Calvin! Catch him!
133	Calvin:	Ralphy! Stop!

134	Vivian:	Ralphy! Come back!
135	Calvin:	Jacob will be disappointed.
136	Vivian:	Does that matter now?
137	Calvin:	Shoot, we lost Ralphy!
138	Vivian:	I'll go home and get his treats. You stay here and try to find him.
139	Calvin:	OK.
140	Note:	(a few minutes later)
141	Vivian:	I got his bowl of treats, food, and some water.
142	Calvin:	Smart.
143	Vivian:	Jacob should be coming with the leash. It took me forever to convince him to get it.
144	Calvin:	No wonder. You were kind of slow.
145	Vivian:	Here comes Jacob!
146	Calvin:	Jacob!
147	Jacob:	Yeah?
148	Calvin:	Hurry up!
149	Jacob:	I'm running!
150	Vivian:	Yeah, right!
151	Jacob:	Let's go find Ralphy.
152	Vivian:	I told you!
153	Jacob:	Uhh, what did you tell me?
154	Calvin:	That we would need the leash.
155	Jacob:	Oh, well…
156	Vivian:	I think I see Ralphy!
157	Calvin:	Where?
158	Vivian:	To your left, he's in the grass field.
159	Jacob:	Run!
160	Vivian:	Come on, Calvin!
161	Calvin:	Coming!
162	Vivian:	Come here, Ralphy. Come here!

163 Ralphy: Woof woof! (barking)

164 Calvin: Bad boy!

165 Vivian: Why did you run away?

166 Jacob: Here's the leash.

167 Vivian: So, for once you agree with us?

168 Jacob: That's right.

169 Calvin: Wow!

170 Ralphy: Woof! (barking)

171 Note: (in a living room)

172 Calvin: Ralphy! Where are you? Ralphy?

173 Ralphy: Woof woof! (barking)

174 Calvin: There you are! Come over here. Good boy. I mean, BAD BOY! Never run away again! (Calvin hits him once and Ralphy squeals)

175 Vivian: Why did Ralphy just squeal?

176 Calvin: 'Cause I hit him, dimwit!

177 Mom: Calvin! That is not a nice word. If I hear you use it again, you'll be grounded for one week. Understand?

178 Calvin: Yes, sir (as he does to a genteman)!

179 Mom: Alright, enough of this foul language. You have to be grounded.

180 Calvin: Mom! Sorry! Please don't ground me! I will behave.

181 Mom: No. You are still grounded for one week.

182 Vivian: Mom, just let him go for now. He's only five. He probably just overheard someone say it once. You can ground him when he hits Ralphy again.

183 Mom: Is that all you think about? Dogs?

184 Vivian: No. I'm just saying. Calvin is only five, and he just probably overheard someone say it. He probably doesn't even know what it means.

185 Mom: Could be. Calvin, thank your sister. She just saved you from getting grounded. Instead, NEVER hit Ralphy again. And think before you speak. Understand?

186 Calvin: Yes, Mom. Thanks, Vivian.

187 Mom   Good. Go play now.

188 Calvin: Okay. Vivian, let's go play ball.

189 Vivian: Sure, I'll be right out.

190 Note: (one month later)

191 Calvin: Hey, Mom? Can I get my own dog?

192 Mom: We already have Ralphy.

193 Calvin: Mom! Vivian said if I learn how to take care of Ralphy well, then I can ask you if I can get one of my own.

194 Mom: Really?

195 Calvin: Yes.

196 Mom: Okay. Vivian?

197 Vivian: Yeah?

198 Mom: Did you tell Calvin he can ask to have a dog if he takes care of Ralphy well?

199 Vivian: Yeah, why?

200 Mom: Never mind.

201 Vivian: Mom, Calvin loves dogs.

202 Mom: I know, but one dog is enough.

203 Vivian: I think it'd be good for Calvin, though.

204 Mom: Okay, Calvin. Let's ask your dad about this.

205 Note: (Dad comes home from work)

206 Calvin: Mom! Dad is here!

207 Mom: Okay.

208 Calvin: Mom, you said you would ask Dad.

209 Mom: Oh right. Sorry. Hey Bruce, Calvin wants to get a dog of his own. Is that alright?

210	Dad:	Sure, why not? He has been good for the past month.
211	Mom:	Are you serious? I thought you were going to stand up for me.
212	Dad:	Really? Well it is just the opposite. I was going to call you to ask you if you could tell Calvin he can get a dog.
213	Mom:	Bruce!
214	Dad:	Sorry! Don't freak out! I'm kidding! Now that I think of it though, I think Calvin would do well with a dog to care for.
215	Mom:	Alright.
216	Calvin:	Awesome, Dad! Thank you!
217	Dad:	You are very welcome.
218	Mom:	When shall we go get one?
219	Dad:	Now!
220	Calvin:	Can I choose?
221	Dad:	Of course!
222	Vivian:	(walks into room) What?
223	Dad:	As long as your sister does not object to your choice.
224	Mom:	But, Bruce, you will help Calvin to take care of the dog. Alright?
225	Dad:	Of course. Don't worry about it, Honey.
226	Mom:	We will see about that.
227	Dad:	Okay. Let's go get his own dog!
228	Mom:	Where?
229	Dad:	Where do you think?
230	Mom:	Petsmart.
231	Dad:	Right!

SKIT 8

CAMPING STORY

2   Sarah: Mom, can we go camping?

3   Mom: Sure. Where do you want to go?

4   Sarah: I was thinking the Rocky Mountains. You know, in Colorado.

5   Mom: Really?

6   Sarah: Yeah, why?

7   Mom: That was where I was thinking too.

8   Sarah: Maybe we should really go there, then.

9   Mom: Yeah.

10   Dad: (walks in) What's up with all the chatting?

11   Mom: Oh, Sarah wanted to go camping in the Rocky Mountains in Colorado, and I thought it was a good idea.

12   Dad: Hey, why not? It sounds good to me!

13   Mom: The only problem is gas. Driving from Moab, Utah to Boulder, Colorado will take about six hours, and six hours of driving takes a lot of gas.

14   Dad: It's alright. I was planning to go on a trip anyway. Besides, we never went anywhere during the summer so far. I think we should just go ahead and use the gas.

15	Mom:	Okay, when do we leave?
16	Dad:	When do you want to go, Sarah?
17	Sarah:	Tomorrow.
18	Dad:	Tomorrow it is. Sarah, go pack up right now. I think we'll leave at dawn.
19	Mom:	Are you sure?
20	Dad:	Of course I'm sure. There's only three weeks of summer left.
21	Mom:	Okay. We better get to bed early then.
22	Dad:	Right.
23	Note:	(At dawn)
24	Dad:	Wake up, Sarah.
25	Sarah:	I was awake for half an hour.
26	Dad:	Really? How come?
27	Sarah:	I was so excited.
28	Dad:	Wow. I never knew someone would get so excited for a long car ride.
29	Sarah:	Dad, you know what I mean.
30	Dad:	I do. I'm just teasing you.
31	Mom:	Stop chatting. We have to leave right now.
32	Dad:	Are you ready, Sarah?
33	Sarah:	Yeah.
34	Dad:	What are we waiting for? Let's go!
35	Mom:	That'd be a good idea if we don't want spend the whole day driving.
36	Dad:	Right.
37	Sarah:	I'll be waiting out in the car.
38	Mom:	Alright.
39	Note:	(In the car)
40	Dad:	Everyone has everything they need?
41	Mom:	Wait, I forgot my ATM card.

42	Dad:	Well, you better go get it. Here are the keys.
43	Mom:	Thanks.
44	Dad:	Sarah, do you have all the things you need?
45	Sarah:	I'm sure I do.
46	Dad:	Alright.
47	Mom:	Okay. Let's go!
48	Dad:	Finally! It took us an hour to confirm that we had everything.
49	Mom:	Oh, well. We're on our way now.
50	Dad:	So, Sarah, what do you want to do in the mountains?
51	Sarah:	Hike around, explore, play in creeks, and maybe visit Boulder or something.
52	Mom:	Sarah, how do you know all about this place?
53	Sarah:	We had a research project in school a few months back.
54	Dad:	Wow, I think Sarah really deserves this trip.
55	Mom:	Yeah. I just never really thought Sarah would be interested in camping.
56	Dad:	Me neither.
57	Sarah:	Now you do.
58	Mom:	Yes. We can go more often if you like it this time!
59	Sarah:	Great. I'd love that but I'm going to go to sleep now. I'm tired.
60	Dad:	You should be! You woke up quite early today.
61	Note:	(Rocky Mountains)
62	Dad:	Sarah, wake up!
63	Sarah:	Why?
64	Dad:	Why do you think? We're here!
65	Sarah:	Already? I feel like I fell asleep minutes ago.
66	Dad:	No, it's been a good few hours! I'm glad to see that you got some good sleep.

67	Sarah:	Yeah, me too. I feel so refreshed.
68	Dad:	We already got checked in and all that good stuff. We just need to set up the tent.
69	Sarah:	Cool. When are we setting up the tent?
70	Dad:	Right now, I guess.
71	Mom:	Sarah! Can you help me set up the tent?
72	Sarah:	Awesome!
73	Note:	(Setting up a tent)
74	Mom:	Sarah, will you grab that corner and hammer it down?
75	Sarah:	Yeah.
76	Mom:	Hey, Dan, get the side next to Sarah and do the same.
77	Dad:	Which one?
78	Mom:	Doesn't matter. Any side. I'll do the rest.
79	Dad:	Okay.
80	Mom:	Well, the tent is all set up, and so now we need to get settled in.
81	Sarah:	I love this part.
82	Dad:	Brittany, let's let Sarah put her stuff in first.
83	Mom:	Sure.
84	Sarah:	Cool. Which one should I sleep in?
85	Mom:	Pick whichever one you want, and set your air mattress in there.
86	Sarah:	Thanks.
87	Mom:	Oh, but don't blow up the mattress yet.
88	Sarah:	Why not?
89	Mom:	We're going into Boulder this afternoon and we're going to get an air pump.
90	Sarah:	We don't already have one?
91	Mom:	We forgot it at home.

92	Sarah:	Oh, okay. Jeez, Mom, trying to get me even more anxious?
93	Mom:	Sorry.
94	Sarah:	It's okay. I was just joking.
95	Mom:	Now remember, don't start to mock your mother.
96	Sarah:	Of course, I won't.
97	Mom:	Good. I'm proud of you, Sarah.
98	Sarah:	Thanks.
99	Dad:	Hey, Sarah, do you mind if you move out of the entrance for a while? I've got a big bag coming through.
100	Sarah:	Sorry.
101	Dad:	It's alright.
102	Note:	(After setting up the tent)
103	Mom:	So, Dan, should we go into Boulder right now?
104	Dad:	Yeah, I think we should, before it gets any darker.
105	Mom:	Why don't we just go down there and have dinner while we're at it?
106	Dad:	Good idea.
107	Sarah:	Have you guys been here before?
108	Dad:	Your mom and I came here about three years before you were born.
109	Sarah:	Oh. I guess I missed it.
110	Dad:	It's okay, you're here now.
111	Sarah:	Yep. I guess the important thing is that I'm here right now.
112	Mom:	That's right. Sarah, sometimes you can be very smart.
113	Sarah:	That's because I inherited your genes.
114	Mom:	Really? Thanks.
115	Sarah:	Or maybe it was Dad I got it from.

116 Dad: Bingo! In our family, I was the smart one.

117 Mom: You wish.

118 Dad: Why, are you jealous that you aren't smart?

119 Mom: Dan, stop teasing me.

120 Sarah: Come on. Let's go!

121 Mom: Oh, yes. We should. We totally forgot about Boulder talking about smartness.

122 Dad: Hey, at least you know that.

123 Mom: Dan, stop it!

124 Note: (In the car)

125 Dad: Everyone aboard?

126 Mom: Yes!

127 Sarah: Yes, sir!

128 Dad: Sarah, how do you like this so far?

129 Sarah: Great. I love the air here.

130 Dad: We have fresh air in Utah too.

131 Sarah: Maybe it's because we were stuck in the car for so long.

132 Dad: Probably. So, where do you want to go eat?

133 Sarah: Not a fast-food restaurant, but a cheap one.

134 Dad: Which one is that?

135 Sarah: You probably know better than me because you've been here before.

136 Dad: Sarah, things change. When you were first born, there was no such thing as a movie theater in Moab.

137 Sarah: That is weird.

138 Dad: We'll probably have to ask locals for our way around.

139 Mom: That works.

140 Sarah: I'm tired again.

141 Mom: It's probably because of the high altitude here.

142 Sarah: Probably.

143 Mom: Hey, Sarah, don't sleep.

144 Sarah: Why not?

145 Dad: You might end up staying up the whole night.

146 Mom: He's right. We were on a trip to Australia once and we stayed up because we wanted to, and slept when we wanted to—but that was a bad idea because it was so hard to stay awake during the day even after a few days.

147 Dad: Exactly. Make sure you're awake when the sun is up.

148 Sarah: You guys went everywhere without me.

149 Mom: Don't worry. We'll go many places with you from now on.

150 Sarah: Thanks, that's very comforting.

151 Dad: We'll be in Boulder in about ten minutes.

152 Mom: Already?

153 Dad: Yes. I guess you were really in your conversation.

154 Mom: Wow. That was fast, wasn't it Sarah?

155 Sarah: Yeah.

156 Dad: I see a Mexican restaurant. Do you want to go there, Sarah?

157 Sarah: What's the name?

158 Dad: Hold on. I need to get a little closer.

159 Sarah: Okay.

160 Dad: It's called Margarita.

161 Sarah: Yes! Dad, let's go!

162 Dad: Ok. Brittany, are you alright with it?

163 Mom: Sure. I'm up for anything.

164 Dad: Good.

165 Note: (At Margarita)

166 Jenny: Hello, what may I get you today?

167 Dad: Could we get one chicken burrito, one steak burrito, and one quesadilla?

168 Jenny: Sure. Anything to drink?

169 Dad: Water's fine.

170 Jenny: Okay.

171 Dad: Alright. Do you guys take American Express here?

172 Jenny: Yes we do.

173 Dad: That's good.

174 Jenny: OK. You guys have a nice meal.

175 Mom: Thank you.

176 Sarah: This tastes really good.

177 Dad: Everything tastes good if you eat it once in a while.

178 Mom: I agree. Let's finish up so we can go get the air pump.

179 Dad: Okay.

180 Sarah: I wish I had more time to sit and relax during this meal.

181 Mom: Camping isn't always comfortable.

182 Dad: Definitely. Or warm.

183 Sarah: I got the point!

184 Mom: Sarah, no need to yell.

185 Sarah: Sorry.

186 Note: (Getting the pump)

187 Dad: Which one to choose?

188 Jeff: (worker) Are you guys finding everything alright today?

189 Mom: Actually, we're looking for an air pump to use for air mattresses.

190 Jeff: Well, what you are staring at is pretty much all we have.

191	Dad:	I know, but we're looking for a good deal.
192	Jeff:	Oh, I see. Well this one here is our best-selling one, so we lowered the price. It's usually fifty six, but it's on sale for twenty two now.
193	Dad:	Wow! That's quite a sale! Hey, Sarah, do you think we should get this one?
194	Sarah:	I don't know. Don't ask me. I don't know anything about air pumps.
195	Dad:	Hey, Jeff, does this air pump work alright?
196	Jeff:	It's fantastic!
197	Dad:	Well, Brittany, I think we should get this one.
198	Mom:	Okay, well, we better hurry up because it's getting dark.
199	Dad:	Alright, we'll take this.
200	Jeff:	Great. I can help you here at register six.
201	Note:	(In the car on the way back)
202	Dad:	Wow, it looks like we got ourselves a great deal.
203	Mom:	Yeah, I guess, but that guy... Jeff... seemed over energetic.
204	Dad:	I think that's how he is.
205	Sarah:	Hey, Dad, what if the air pump doesn't work?
206	Dad:	Sarah, don't worry. I told Jeff that if this doesn't work, I would go back to the store and return it.
207	Mom:	What did he say about it?
208	Dad:	Jeff said, "Go on ahead."
209	Mom:	Looks like he was pretty confident.
210	Dad:	Sarah, there's nothing to worry about.
211	Sarah:	Do we get a refund?
212	Mom:	I don't know why you should care, Sarah.
213	Dad:	Hey, Sarah, don't worry. We'll get a refund.
214	Sarah:	Alright. Just wondering.

215	Note:	(Three days later…)
216	Dad:	Hey, Sarah, wake up.
217	Sarah:	Why?
218	Dad:	We're going somewhere really exciting today.
219	Sarah:	Where?
220	Dad:	Elitch's. It'll take a little while to get there so we have to leave right now. Oh, by the way, pack your bag.
221	Sarah:	Why?
222	Dad:	We're going back to Moab straight from Elitch's.
223	Sarah:	Really?
224	Dad:	Yeah. Sarah, school starts in two and a half weeks.
225	Sarah:	Wow, that went fast. I guess I had a pretty good time.
226	Dad:	You sure did.
227	Sarah:	I'll be out in ten minutes.
228	Dad:	Okay.
229	Note:	(In the car for Elitch's)
230	Mom:	Sarah, what do you think of Elitch's?
231	Sarah:	I don't know. I don't even know what it is.
232	Mom:	Dan, you didn't tell her what it even was?
233	Dad:	Oh, I totally forgot. It's Colorado's biggest amusement park.
234	Sarah:	Really? I haven't been on a roller coaster in years!
235	Dad:	Hey, want to practice screaming?
236	Mom:	No.
237	Dad:	Don't look at me like that. I was just joking.
238	Mom:	Oh. I thought you were serious.
239	Dad:	Oh, no. I definitely do not want to lose my hearing today.
240	Sarah:	I know. No one does.

241 Mom: Hopefully.

242 Note: (at Moab)

243 Sarah: Thanks for taking me camping, Mom and Dad.

244 Mom: You're welcome.

245 Dad: We should do this again next year.

246 Sarah: I don't know if Mom would like to.

247 Mom: What are you talking about? Of course I'd like to!

248 Dad: Well, there's already one thing on our calendar for next summer.

249 Sarah: Right.

SKIT 9

TRIP TO ITALY

2	Elizabeth:	Mom!
3	Mom:	Yes?
4	Elizabeth:	When are we going to go to Italy?
5	Mom:	During summer break.
6	Ralf:	SUMMER BREAK!?
7	Dad:	Yes, it's that or nothing.
8	Ralf:	That's like forever from now! But where are you going to get the tickets?
9	Kevin:	It is!
10	Mom:	Calm down! We need to get the tickets.
11	Zoe:	I want to go.
12	Mom:	The younger the kid, the calmer they are! And Ralf, we need to get the tickets online.
13	Dad:	I know. Ralf and Elizabeth are 12, and they are really fussy!
14	Elizabeth:	No, we're not!
15	Dad:	Kevin is six, and Zoe is three!
16	McKenna:	Yeah!
17	Dad:	And McKenna is only one and a half years old!

18	Ralf:	I just noticed, that Elizabeth and I are twelve, and half of twelve is six, and Kevin is six, and half of six is three, and Zoe is three, and half of three is one and a half and McKenna is one and a half!
19	Mom:	You didn't notice that before?
20	Elizabeth:	We didn't.
21	Ralf:	Yeah, we didn't.
22	Dad:	Honestly, I didn't know either.
23	Mom:	WOW! I thought everyone knew, so I didn't tell anyone.
24	Kevin:	Back to the discussion on our trip!
25	Mom:	SUMMER.
26	Kids:	Okay (grumbles).
27	Note:	(Summer)
28	Ralf:	So, we're leaving tomorrow?
29	Mom:	Yes, we are.
30	Dad:	Yes, we finally are. We all have been waiting for this for a long time.
31	Ralf:	It was the longest spring in my life.
32	Elizabeth:	I've been waiting for this my whole life!
33	Zoe:	I'm excited!
34	Elizabeth:	Me too! This is going to be so fun!
35	Ralf:	Ditto!
36	Zoe:	What's "ditto"?
37	Elizabeth:	It means "same here."
38	Zoe:	Oh, that makes sense now.
39	Note:	(Packing for the trip)
40	Kevin:	Mom?!
41	Mom:	Yes?
42	Kevin:	So, we are going to stay in Italy for a month?

43	Mom:	Yea, one month.
44	Elizabeth:	That sounds serious.
45	Dad:	In a sense.
46	Elizabeth:	We probably need lots of clothes!
47	Ralf:	Good point!
48	Kevin:	How many pairs of underwear, shirts, pants and socks do I need to pack?
49	Zoe:	Can someone help me get packed?
50	McKenna:	Bubba?
51	Elizabeth:	Ralf!
52	Ralf:	What?!
53	Elizabeth:	After you pack, as Mom said, we need to help Zoe and McKenna.
54	Ralf:	So?
55	Elizabeth:	Do you want to help Zoe or McKenna?
56	Ralf:	Zoe.
57	Elizabeth:	Why?
58	Ralf:	She can talk.
59	Elizabeth:	That's funny.
60	Ralf:	I can understand her.
61	Elizabeth:	I guess I'm helping McKenna, who can't talk.
62	Ralf:	Sounds good.
63	Mom:	Elizabeth? Ralf?
64	Elizabeth:	Yeah?
65	Ralf:	Yeah?
66	Mom:	Pack three shirts, and three shorts. Bring two pants, and three long sleeves, and two jackets. And, seven undergarments.
67	Ralf:	So that's for all of us, right?
68	Mom:	Right. I will help Kevin pack. You guys help Zoe and McKenna. You decide who helps who.

69	Elizabeth:	We already did. Ralf will help Zoe, and I will help McKenna.
70	Mom:	Okay. Elizabeth! One more thing, with McKenna, pack her "bubbah."
71	Elizabeth:	Bubbah? Ah, McKenna's blanket! Okay.
72	Ralf:	Wow, 3 of basically every thing!
73	Elizabeth:	And 7 of you know what.
74	Ralf:	Right.
75	Note:	(After Elizabeth and Ralf packed)
76	Ralf:	Zoe!
77	Zoe:	Ya?
78	Ralf:	You need to pack.
79	Zoe:	And you are going to help, right?
80	Ralf:	Yeah.
81	Zoe:	I want this shirt, this one, and that one, the red one, the blue one, the one in the back, the one in front of you, and the one to your right....
82	Elizabeth:	I think McKenna likes this shirt, do you McKenna?
83	McKenna:	Yeah.
84	Elizabeth:	How about this one?
85	McKenna:	Ne.
86	Elizabeth:	This?
87	McKenna:	Ne.
88	Elizabeth:	How about this?
89	McKenna:	Yeah...
90	Note:	(Going to the airport)
91	McKenna:	Yeah!
92	Elizabeth:	Funny McKenna.
93	Ralf:	How much longer to the airport?
94	Dad:	Why?

95	Ralf:	According to Zoe, she's getting carsick.
96	Dad:	Around 10 minutes?
97	Zoe:	I can handle that!
98	Ralf:	Thank God.
99	Elizabeth:	Seriously. We would probably have to clean it up.
100	Dad:	Probably. But then again, we might.
101	Mom:	Right. It's not like we make you guys do everything.
102	Ralf:	I guess.
103	Kevin:	Mom?
104	Mom:	Yes?
105	Kevin:	Did you bring Candy?
106	Mom:	Who's Candy?
107	Kevin:	The bear with candy hearts on the palms and the feet.
108	Mom:	Yes, I brought her, but those aren't candy.
109	Kevin:	What are they?
110	Elizabeth:	They're just hearts.
111	Kevin:	Then, I will rename Candy to Hearts.
112	Elizabeth:	Hearts is a good name!
113	Ralf:	I like it.
114	McKenna:	Yeah.
115	Zoe:	I like it too!
116	Note:	(At the airport)
117	Mom:	Take your shoes off and put them in the tubs. Then put the tub on the conveyor belt. Elizabeth, help McKenna and Ralf, help Zoe.
118	Elizabeth:	Sure.
119	Ralf:	Okay.
120	Elizabeth:	McKenna, sit!

121	McKenna:	No.
122	Elizabeth:	Sit on my lap then.
123	McKenna:	Yeah.
124	Ralf:	Take your shoes off, Zoe!
125	Zoe:	I Can't.
126	Ralf:	Okay. I will help you.
127	Mom:	Good…
128	Dad:	Come over here and put your shoes on.
129	Mom:	Elizabeth, Ralf, you know.
130	Ralf:	We do know.
131	Elizabeth:	We do.
132	Dad:	Come here, and put your bags on the conveyor belt!
133	Mom:	Elizabeth, Ralf…
134	Elizabeth:	Mom, it would be easier if you just said "you know."
135	Mom:	Okay, I will just say "you know" from now on.
136	Ralf:	Okay, fine with me.
137	Alex:	There is something in the red bag that we need to check.
138	Mom:	That would be the family bag.
139	Kevin:	Is there something bad going on?
140	Dad:	No, it's just that they want to check.
141	Alex:	So, may I check it?
142	Mom:	Sure. But what is it?
143	Alex:	We'll have to see!
144	Mom:	Okay.
145	Alex:	It is toothpaste!
146	Mom:	So, will we have to leave that here?
147	Alex:	Let me see how many ounces it is.
148	Dad:	It should be one ounce.

149	Alex:	Then you are fine!
150	Dad:	Thanks.
151	Alex:	That was nothing.
152	Kevin:	Phew.
153	Mom:	You guys hungry?
154	Elizabeth:	Yeah…
155	Ralf:	Starving!
156	Kevin:	Me too.
157	Zoe:	Can I have something to eat?
158	McKenna:	Yeah.
159	Mom:	Let's go grab something to eat and eat while we wait for the plane.
160	Dad:	Sure.
161	Mom:	What do you guys want?
162	Ralf:	Umm…teriyaki?
163	Elizabeth:	Teriyaki!
164	Kevin:	Same.
165	Zoe:	Me too.
166	McKenna:	Teri!
167	Dad:	Okay. I'll be right back.
168	Note:	(Waiting for the airplane)
169	Elizabeth:	Yum.
170	Ralf:	I like teriyaki.
171	Zoe:	Me too.
172	Kevin:	I've had it before. I like it a lot.
173	McKenna:	Yeah.
174	Dad:	Good enough.
175	Mom:	Not bad.
176	Kevin:	AIRPLANE!
177	Mom:	Will you go throw this away?
178	Dad:	Sure.

179	Mom:	Elizabeth and Ralf!
180	Elizabeth:	Hmm?
181	Ralf:	Yes?
182	Mom:	Get yours and your sisters' passports and tickets out! You guys know which ones I'm talking about.
183	Ralf:	We do.
184	Note:	(Italy)
185	Elizabeth :	Are we really here?
186	Dad:	We are all finally here. We survived the long plane ride.
187	Kevin:	I can't believe we're actually here.
188	Ralf:	I want pasta, pizza and food.
189	Mom:	Let's go get some food.
190	Kevin:	I want pasta!
191	Mom:	So you want pasta and I want Italian pizza.
192	Elizabeth:	Pizza please!
193	Mom:	Ralf, do you want pizza or pasta?
194	Ralf:	Pasta. Elizabeth, let's share.
195	Elizabeth:	Sure. I want both pasta and pizza. We can all share.
196	Dad:	Pizza.
197	Mom:	So we've got three (3) pastas and three (3) pizzas?
198	Dad:	What about Zoe and McKenna?
199	Mom:	Let's order a pasta for them.
200	Dad:	That'll be best.
201	Note:	(Eating)
202	Zoe:	Mmmm.
203	Elizabeth:	I like pasta best.
204	Ralf:	I don't know, I'm just too hungry!

205	Mom:	Glad you're enjoying it! You'll have to eat this the whole month!
206	Kevin:	Fine with me!
207	Note:	(Going to the hotel)
208	McKenna:	(gibberish) Uhh buah!
209	Dad:	Tired?
210	Elizabeth:	Yeah, totally.
211	Zoe:	I'm sleepy.
212	Mom:	What do you guys want now?
213	Elizabeth:	A shower then bed.
214	Mom:	Well, Zoe and McKenna are asleep.
215	Dad:	The little ones must be tired after such a trip.
216	Ralf:	We are still fine.
217	Mom:	I'm glad you guys are tough, Elizabeth and Ralf.
218	Ralf:	Yes we are, don't worry about us.
219	Note:	(At hotel)
220	Ralf:	Now that we can all kind of speak Italian, I think checking in will be easier.
221	Elizabeth:	You know what? I worked so hard on learning Italian that I think my head is going to burst!
222	Dad:	Well, Elizabeth, it'll be worth it. Besides, your head can't burst.
223	Note:	(After checking in)
224	Elizabeth:	I'm tired. As soon as we get to our rooms, I'm going to get ready for bed, explore the room a little and then sleep.
225	Ralf:	Me too.
226	Mom:	I'm tired, too.
227	Ralf:	I'd like to rest until late tomorrow.
228	Mom:	I think we can do that.
229	Dad:	We are going to hang around the city tomorrow.

230	Note:	(In the room)
231	Elizabeth:	WOW! I'm not tired anymore! This room is amazing!
232	Mom:	We got a good room.
233	Ralf:	It's so luxurious!
234	Elizabeth:	It is! I'm going to take a shower in the luxury bathroom and sleep.
235	Ralf:	Me too.
236	Dad:	Remember, there is only one shower even if this is a luxurious place!!
237	Elizabeth:	Can I go first?
238	Ralf:	Sure.
239	Note:	(After showering and getting ready for bed)
240	Mom:	Go to sleep!
241	Ralf:	Mom, we didn't even choose our beds!
242	Mom:	You're right, Ralf!
243	Dad:	Kevin, Ralf and I will sleep in the small room.
244	Mom:	Okay. Well, I will sleep with the girls in the big room.
245	Elizabeth	Okay, us girls will sleep together.
246	Ralf	OK. You do that.
247	Mom:	Well, Zoe, Kevin and McKenna are asleep in the small room already.
248	Ralf:	Okay. So we should take Zoe and McKenna into the big room, right?
249	Dad:	Yup.
250	Elizabeth:	Ralf, go get Zoe. I will get McKenna.
251	Ralf:	Okay. Zoe isn't heavy, is she, Mom?
252	Mom:	She should be a little heavier since she is sleeping, but she shouldn't be too heavy.
253	Ralf:	Okay.

254	Note:	(In the room, getting ready to sleep)
255	Elizabeth:	Okay. I will dress McKenna and brush her teeth.
256	Ralf:	I will do the same for Zoe.
257	Elizabeth:	Where are McKenna's pajamas?
258	Ralf:	In Zoe's bag. Here!
259	Elizabeth:	Thanks.
260	Ralf:	And here, Zoe's pajamas.
261	Elizabeth:	I got McKenna in her pajamas.
262	Ralf:	I've got Zoe in hers.
263	Elizabeth:	I like brushing McKenna's teeth with the little toothbrush.
264	Ralf:	Well, here it is.
265	Elizabeth:	Open, McKenna!
266	Ralf:	You do know that she's asleep, don't you?
267	Elizabeth:	Well, yeah.
268	Mom:	Getting it, guys?
269	Ralf:	Yeah.
270	Elizabeth:	I will sleep with McKenna.
271	Mom	Zoe.
272	Elizabeth:	Goodnight!
273	Ralf:	You too.
274	Note:	(Elizabeth is quiet)
275	Mom	Liz?
276	Elizabeth:	Too…tired.
277	Note:	(Morning)
278	Dad:	Today, we'll look around Rome!
279	Elizabeth:	Cool!
280	Mom:	We're going to visit Campo de Fiori.
281	Kevin:	What will we see there?

282	Mom:	I read that there is a market everyday except on Sundays, and today is Monday. I think we will also see the Spanish Steps.
283	Ralf:	Whatever you say!
284	Note:	(Spanish Steps)
285	Mom:	Look at that! There is a boat shaped fountain!
286	Dad:	There are coins in there! Do you guys want to throw some in?
287	Zoe:	Ya.
288	Mom:	I think everyone should do it, including Dad and me.
289	Dad:	Sounds fun.
290	Ralf:	Ready, aim, throw! Oh yeah! I made it into the center!
291	Elizabeth:	Ready, aim, throw! Cool! I made it onto the center!
292	Mom:	I didn't do anything special.
293	Dad:	Me neither.
294	Kevin:	Mine went past the center!
295	Zoe:	Mine's there in the front!
296	Mom:	Tomorrow, let's go to the Naples beaches!
297	Dad:	A beach sounds like a refreshing idea!
298	Elizabeth:	I want to go to the beach.
299	Mom:	Then we'll go!
300	Kevin:	(At Naples beaches) Crowd!
301	Mom:	I believe the crowd is half the fun.
302	Dad:	I agree!
303	Ralf:	(At Venice) Mom, can we please go down the Grand Canal?
304	Elizabeth:	I want to go down the canal.

305	Dad:	Since we are leaving tomorrow, let's let the kids do what they want.
306	Mom:	Okay.
307	Kevin:	Canal! Canal! Canal!
308	Dad:	We got it Kevin!
309	Mom:	(Going down the Grand Canal) In Venice, where we are right now, you play on the water, not on the city streets.
310	Ralf:	Cool! I would like that, but not on a snowy winter day.
311	Dad:	(At the hotel, checking out) Our trip is over. Was that month fun?
312	Elizabeth:	Totally!

UNIT 4

SKIT 1

PE CLASS

2	Meredith:	Oh, no, PE next.
3	Renee:	It'll be fine. Nothing was too bad before.
4	Maylan:	We're running the mile today!
5	Meredith:	What did I say, Renee?
6	Renee:	Yes, you were right.
7	Maylan:	Come on, let's go change.
8	Meredith:	I guess. It's always better if you don't get in trouble.
9	Renee:	I have to beat my time from last year. Last year, I ran it in five minutes and twenty three seconds (00:05:23).
10	Meredith:	Wow…that's amazing. I ran it in just under eight minutes.
11	Maylan:	No way, me too! High five!
12	Renee:	Coach blew the whistle. Let's go.
13	Mr. Babotto	As you all very well know, the mile run is today!
14	Maylan:	(Quietly) You're the only one excited.
15	Mr. Babotto	You'll start on "GO." On your mark, get set, GO! (Kids start running)
16	Meredith:	Do you know what's great though, Renee?

17	Renee:	What?
18	Meredith:	We actually only run half a mile. In middle school you run a full mile.
19	Renee:	I don't care.
20	Maylan:	Cause you like running.
21	Mr Babotto:	Go change. Class dismissed.
22	Maylan:	That was TIRING.
23	Renee:	But I did beat my best score! I've been training for a whole year! I got five minutes and fourteen seconds (00:05:14)!
24	Meredith:	Hey, I beat my time too! Six minutes and twelve seconds (00:06:12)! Did you say you were training for the mile?
25	Renee:	No, dummy! For marathons and stuff!
26	Maylan:	Oh! I was going to say…
27	Meredith:	Anyway, good thing we only have to do that twice a year.
28	Maylan:	Twice a year is still a lot.
29	Meredith:	I agree.
30	Maylan:	So, what do you guys have next?
31	Meredith:	Science.
32	Renee:	Have fun with that. I get to go cool off in band.
33	Maylan:	Sweet! Is the band room cold or something?
34	Renee:	Yeah, I don't think there's any heating.
35	Maylan:	That must suck in the winter.
36	Renee:	There are pros and cons to everything.
37	Meredith:	Well said.
38	Renee:	Thanks. Anyway, I'll see you guys later.
39	Maylan:	Okay, see you later.
40	Meredith:	Bye.

SKIT 2

MAKING FRIENDS ON A BUS

2	Charlie:	Hey, do you mind if I sit next to you?
3	Alex:	No, not at all.
4	Charlie:	Sorry. All the other seats are taken.
5	Alex:	Oh, it's alright.
6	Charlie:	Thanks. Where are you headed?
7	Alex:	I'm going to drop by my friend's house.
8	Charlie:	Nice! Where are you getting off?
9	Alex:	Table Mesa and Broadway.
10	Charlie:	Really?
11	Alex:	Yeah.
12	Charlie:	Me too.
13	Alex:	That's sick! Do you live nearby?
14	Charlie:	Yeah, straight up the sidewalk and on the left.
15	Alex:	Oh, my friend lives a little down the sidewalk. It takes about fifteen minutes to walk, but I like walking.
16	Charlie:	I bet Boulder has a great view.
17	Alex:	Yeah, that's why I love coming here.
18	Charlie:	Do you live in Colorado?
19	Alex:	Oh, no. I live in New York, but I'm on vacation.

20	Charlie:	Wow, I see. A big change in atmosphere?
21	Alex:	Oh, definitely.
22	Charlie:	I've been to New York a few times. It's really crowded, but I like it there for some reason.
23	Alex:	Really? I don't like it there too much, but my dad has a job there at the moment.
24	Charlie:	So you prefer quieter places?
25	Alex:	Yes, I really like Boulder. My uncle is here, too, and I love visiting him. I try to go visit every other year.
26	Charlie:	Did you come here alone?
27	Alex:	No, I came here with my parents. They're hiking a trail in the mountains.
28	Charlie:	Do you have any brothers or sisters?
29	Alex:	No, I'm an only child.
30	Charlie:	Oh, by the way, my name is Charlie. I go to school here, in Boulder. What's your name?
31	Alex:	Alex. Nice to meet you.
32	Charlie:	Do you have friends here?
33	Alex:	Yes, I have one.
34	Charlie:	What's your friend's name?
35	Alex:	Her name is Veronica Miller. I met her two summers ago at my cousin's birthday party.
36	Charlie:	Really? I may know her then!
37	Alex:	Well, here's our stop. Maybe I'll see you around. Hey, by the way, what's your number? Maybe we can keep in touch?
38	Charlie:	Oh, yeah. My number is three oh three, four nine seven, eight seven two one (303-497-8721).
39	Alex:	Sweet. Mine is seven one eight, four seven nine, one eight five four (718-479-1854).

40	Charlie:	Awesome. Do you text?
41	Alex:	Yes. Well, text me if you ever want to hang out.
42	Charlie:	Definitely. Bye!

Skit 3

HOW MUCH CAN YOU EAT?

2	Michael:	Hey, Simon. Are you playing tee-ball this summer?
3	Simon:	I think so. My dad is coaching a team.
4	Michael:	That must be fun having your dad as the coach.
5	Simon:	It is, but he doesn't always let me bat first.
6	Michael:	Oh, that's a bummer. Does he let you play first base?
7	Simon:	Not always.
8	Michael:	Oh, why not?
9	Simon:	He said that we have to be fair to the other kids.
10	Michael:	They probably want to play first base, too.
11	Simon:	But he does take me out for pizza after the games.
12	Michael:	My dad takes me to McDonald's after practice.
13	Simon:	Do you get a Happy Meal?
14	Michael:	No, they aren't big enough. I eat ten chicken nuggets.
15	Simon:	Impressive. When I go to McDonald's, I just get a BigMac and I'm good.
16	Michael:	I get chicken nuggets, a double cheeseburger, and some fries.

17	Simon:	Wow!
18	Michael:	Yeah. I probably could eat more if it wasn't McDonald's.
19	Simon:	What do you mean?
20	Michael:	I mean, if I was at a buffet, I could probably eat a lot more.
21	Simon:	I see. I love buffets.
22	Michael:	Yeah. Every time I go, I eat way too much.
23	Simon:	I usually get around five dishes.
24	Michael:	I get a plate for every food.
25	Simon:	That is a lot of food. No wonder you are so tall.
26	Michael:	Yeah. Hans, what did you bring for lunch today?
27	Hans:	A turkey sandwich, chips, and an apple. Oh, and some homemade cookies. What about you?
28	Michael:	My mom packed the wrong lunch for me. It's something green.
29	Hans:	That looks like a salad.
30	Michael:	I don't really like salads or peaches.
31	Hans:	It looks like you better go buy some lunch. Do you know what the menu is for today?
32	Michael:	Tacos. Gross.
33	Hans:	I love tacos. If you get tacos, I'll trade you.
34	Michael:	That would be great. Thanks, Hans. That is really nice of you.
35	Hans:	No problem. But I'm keeping one of the cookies.
36	Michael:	You got it.
37	Hans:	Here's the sandwich, chips, apple and cookie.
38	Michael:	Thanks! What kind of cookies are they?
39	Simon:	They look like Snickerdoodles. They're classic.
40	Michael:	(Takes a bite) Wow! These are delicious! Did you make these?

41 Hans: No, but my sister did.

42 Michael: Wow, she's a great cook.

43 Simon: Really? (Lunges for cookies)

44 Michael: Dude! Give me my cookies!

45 Simon: (Grabs a cookie) Just one.

46 Michael: Alright. Just one.

Skit 4

I WANT MY PHONE

2   Note: (In Josh's room)

3   Josh: Hey, Mom, can I get a phone?

4   Mom: Why? I thought you said you wanted a new trumpet for your birthday.

5   Josh: Well, all the kids at my school have phones, and I think they are awesome. I also think that it's time I need one.

6   Mom: Are you sure everyone has one? Also, do you think the kids are awesome because they have a phone, or do you think the phones are awesome?

7   Josh: I mean the phones are awesome! Not the kids. There are so many nice ones out there! There is the...

8   Mom: (Cuts Josh off) Okay, I don't need to know about all the different types of phones out there. Now answer my other question. Does everyone have one?

9   Josh: Yes. Actually, no. But the majority do.

10   Mom: I want you to say it more reasonably.

11   Josh: Yes, Mom.

12   Mom: As for the phone, I need to talk to Dad first, okay?

13   Josh: Alright.

14	Mom:	Go practice trumpet now.
15	Josh:	I don't think I can concentrate on anything now because I'm so excited about the phone.
16	Mom:	That's a problem.
17	Josh:	Yea, please get me one, Mom.
18	Mom:	Maybe. (Turns around and walks out of room)
19	Josh:	Okay.
20	Dad:	(Dad walks in) Hey, Josh, how was your day?
21	Josh:	Not good.
22	Dad:	(look surprised) Why is that?
23	Josh:	Mom won't get me a phone until you agree to get me one.
24	Dad:	Oh, let me talk to Mom about it. (Dad leaves the room)
25	Note:	(Dad comes in again after a short while)
26	Dad:	Come on, let's get you one right now. Mom and I agreed to buy you a phone.
27	Josh:	Really?
28	Dad:	Yeah. Why not?
29	Josh:	Awesome!
30	Note:	(At Costco)
31	Ali:	(Costco worker) How may I help you today, sir?
32	Dad:	Well, I'm trying to get my son a new phone.
33	Ali:	Oh, well that's easy. Come on right over here.
34	Note:	(Go to the phone section)
35	Ali:	What is your name?
36	Josh:	Josh.
37	Ali:	Okay, Josh, here is the collection of phones we have. Pick the one that you would like.
38	Josh:	(Smiling ear to ear and looking at all the phones) Dad, can I get this one?

39	Dad:	Which one is that one?
40	Josh:	The most expensive one.
41	Dad:	How much is it?
42	Josh:	Five hundred dollars.
43	Dad:	(looked shocked) No.
44	Josh:	I was just kidding. I don't want the most expensive one. I want a black Mphone.
45	Dad:	How much would that be?
46	Josh:	I don't know. Ask Ali.
47	Dad:	Excuse me, ma'am.
48	Ali:	Yes?
49	Dad:	How much would the black Mphone be?
50	Ali:	Is Josh continuing a number, or is he starting a new line?
51	Dad:	A new line.
52	Ali:	Okay. That will be fifty ($50) plus tax.
53	Dad:	Great. I'll take this one.
54	Note:	(After purchasing the phone)
55	Josh:	Thanks, Dad.
56	Dad:	You're welcome. Promise me though that you will read two books each week for the rest of the summer, do twenty math problems from your Algebra book each day, and practice your trumpet one hour a day.
57	Josh:	(stares at his Dad in disbelief) You've got to be kidding.
58	Dad:	Yes, I am.
59	Josh:	(laugh) I knew it! Don't scare me like that, Dad!
60	Note:	(Home)
61	Josh:	I'm home, Mom!
62	Mom:	Where from?

63 Josh: Costco.

64 Mom: Did you get a phone?

65 Josh: Yea.

66 Mom: What did you get?

67 Josh: Black Mphone.

68 Mom: What do you say?

69 Josh: Thank you, Mom and Dad.

SKIT 5

WHAT I WANT TO BE

2	Mr. Robins:	Alright, class, tomorrow we will talk about what you want to be when you grow up.
3	Mr. Robins:	So, for the rest of today, I want you to think about what you want to be in the future.
4	Hannah:	What if you don't know?
5	Mr. Robins:	That's why I'm telling you to think about it. I'll give you twenty minutes to do so. Remember, it can be anything, and it can always change.
6	Astoria:	What if I already know?
7	Mr. Robins:	Then you may sit quietly or whisper with a peer.
8	Matt:	What does 'peer' mean?
9	Mr. Robins:	Basically, it means a classmate or a friend.
10	Matt:	Oh, thank you.
11	Mr. Robins:	You're very welcome. Now, quiet everyone.
12	Note:	(Later)
13	Mr. Robins:	Okay, class. Have you decided?
14	Class:	Yes, Mr. Robins.
15	Mr. Robins:	Now, for homework, I'd like you to write a few sentences on why you want to be whatever you said you want to be. Understand?

16	Class:	Yes, Mr. Robins.
17	Mr. Robins:	Good. Well, it's lunch time!
18	Note:	(Next Day)
19	Mr. Robins:	Did everyone do their homework?
20	Class:	Yes.
21	Mr. Robins:	Good. Who wants to share first?
22	Kennedy:	If we share, do we read our paragraphs or just say what we want to be and why?
23	Mr. Robins:	Just say what you want to be and why.
24	Astoria:	I'll go first.
25	Mr. Robins:	Alright!
26	Astoria:	I want to be a model because it sounds fun, and you make a lot of money if you are photogenic, which I think I am. Even one photo can bring in a big income.
27	Mr. Robins:	Excellent! That was a perfect example!
28	Daphne:	May I go next?
29	Mr. Robins:	Of course.
30	Daphne:	I want to be a singer. I would like to become a singer because I love publicity and music is my life.
31	Mr. Robins:	Do you take private lessons?
32	Daphne:	Of course!
33	Mr. Robins:	That's what I thought. Who wants to go next?
34	Brooklyn:	Me.
35	Mr. Robins:	Alright, Brooklyn!
36	Brooklyn:	I want to be an actress. As an actress, you can pretend to be someone you're not, and I think that's neat.
37	Brooklyn:	I want to become rich and famous, like many actresses.

38	Mr. Robins:	That sounds wonderful! If you become an actress, I will be your biggest fan.
39	Brooklyn:	Thank you.
40	Mr. Robins:	Next?
41	Brooklyn:	I'm not done yet!
42	Mr. Robins:	Oh, sorry about that! Go on, please!
43	Brooklyn:	Emma Watson wasn't famous until she was 11.
44	Mr. Robins:	Right. Are you saying that you want to start your career like Emma Watson?
45	Brooklyn:	My point exactly.
46	Mr. Robins:	Wonderful. Is that it?
47	Brooklyn:	I wrote more in my paragraph, as speech is important in a celebrity's life. But those are the main points!
48	Mr. Robins:	Outstanding. Volunteers? Or should I pick?
49	Veronica:	I'll go!
50	Mr. Robins:	What would you like to be?
51	Veronica:	I'm going to be the Princess of Luxembourg.
52	Mr. Robins:	Why is that?
53	Veronica:	A princess would be cool because you don't have to worry about your financial situation, and you're part of the royal family!
54	Mr. Robins:	Sounds like fun, Veronica.
55	Veronica:	I know it will be!
56	Mr. Robins:	Next?
57	Evelyn:	Could I go next, Mr. Robins?
58	Mr. Robins:	Of course, Evelyn!
59	Evelyn:	I would like to be the president's secretary. You get to know the truths about the country that the president might not tell the public.

60	Mr. Robins:	Wow, that's truly an amazing dream! Make it a reality!
61	Evelyn:	Also, you can help the president run the country.
62	Mr. Robins:	Very good.
63	Gina:	Mr. Robins?
64	Mr. Robins:	Yes, Gina?
65	Gina:	The bell rings in two minutes.
66	Mr. Robins:	Oh, wow. Time flies! Thanks, Gina. Everyone, pack up. We'll finish tomorrow.

SKIT 6

FOURSQUARE GAME

2	Note:	(At Alice's house)
3	Alice:	So…what do you guys want to do?
4	Elizabeth:	We can go bowling if you want. I know there's a bowling alley at the university.
5	Presley:	I'm not really in the mood to go anywhere. I'd rather do something at the house.
6	Alice:	Like what?
7	Maria:	Hey, Alice, are we allowed to use the stove and stuff?
8	Alice:	Yeah, why?
9	Maria:	Why don't we cook something?
10	Elizabeth:	Sure! I love cooking!
11	Alice:	I do, too, but we might not have all the ingredients.
12	Maria:	Oh yeah, I forgot about that. Hmm, what else can we do?
13	Presley:	Is everyone okay with Foursquare? I bought a ball the other day.
14	Alice:	Sure! Then I can dominate during school lunch time!

15 Presley: It's beneficial to all of us! We can rule the Foursquare kingdom at school!

16 Elizabeth: Sounds great! I really need to get to A square because I can't do footsies.

17 Alice: Alright! I have chalk in the garage. I'll go get some to draw the squares.

18 Maria: Perfect. Get four colors, Alice.

19 Alice: I will! Where do you guys want to play? There's the basketball court.

20 Elizabeth: Yeah, let's play on the basketball court!

21 Presley: I hope no one is there...

22 Elizabeth: Let's just go check.

23 Maria: Right. That's a good idea.

24 Elizabeth: Okay, we will go first, and you can come later with some chalk.

25 Presley: I will go get a ball from my house and join you guys soon.

26 Elizabeth: Okay.

27 Alice: I'll meet you guys there. Sound good?

28 Friends: Great!

29 Note: (After 5~10 Minutes)

30 Maria: Look! Here come Alice and Presley!

31 Alice: Hey, guys! So I have pink, green, blue, and yellow chalk.

32 Elizabeth: Cool! So I found these squares on the court. They're perfect for Foursquare.

33 Alice: Great. We'll use those then.

34 Maria: Perfect. Let's get started.

35 Presley: Everyone knows how to play, right?

36 Elizabeth: Umm...I think I know how to play but we should go over the rules first.

37	Alice:	Sure. We have four squares in a big square just like we have here. Four people play at a time, one person in each square.
38	Alice:	The person in A square starts and bounces the ball to anyone in the game, and the person that has the ball then passes it to another person.
39	Maria:	And, anyone with the ball can attack anyone by bouncing the ball to the person's square.
40	Maria:	If the ball bounces in your square and it touches the ground again before you catch it, you're out.
41	Maria:	So, you don't have to be in your square when you catch it, though.
42	Alice:	Someone else can catch the ball for them and continue the game.
43	Presley:	When you get out, you go to D square. Then everyone moves up. The object is to get to A square.
44	Maria:	Do I always need to stay in my square?
45	Presley:	Yea, except when you are going outside to get the ball.
46	Alice:	Oh, one more thing. The person in Square A gets to call the type of game you are going to play.
47	Maria:	Like what?
48	Alice:	Like hands, footsies, or ultimate.
49	Presley:	Any questions?
50	Elizabeth:	No, that really cleared things up.
51	Alice:	Let's play!
52	Maria:	Looks like Presley is in A square.
53	Presley:	Sweet. Give me the ball. (Alice hands her the ball) Okay, hands only.
54	Maria:	Okay.

55	Elizabeth:	Fantastic! I'm great with my hands.
56	Presley:	Oh, and no outs on serves.
57	Maria:	What does that mean again?
58	Presley:	It means that you can't get out by a serve. In other words, I can't get you out when I start.
59	Maria:	Oh, okay.
60	Presley:	Here goes. (Serves ball to Elizabeth)
61	Elizabeth:	Whoa!
62	Alice:	You have to be prepared!
63	Elizabeth:	Well...sorry~! (Bounces ball to Maria)
64	Maria:	That was out!
65	Elizabeth:	Was not!
66	Alice:	Was too!
67	Maria:	Told you! Elizabeth, you are now in D square, my friend.
68	Presley:	I like how there's four people. We can't ever get out of the game.
69	Elizabeth:	Serve the ball, Presley!!
70	Presley:	Okay! (serves the ball to Alice)
71	Alice:	Let's get Presley out since she's in A square!
72	Maria:	Elizabeth, you're lucky. No one's trying to get you out.
73	Elizabeth:	I know, I know. I'm lucky. D square is like the pressure free square.
74	Alice:	Definitely.

Skit 7

TRIP TO MT. FUJI

2   Trevor: Hey, Mom? Isn't Mt. Fuji a famous landmark in Japan?

3   Mom: Yes, it is, and you know we're going to be heading up there tomorrow.

4   Trevor: Awesome!

5   Amy: Yeah!

6   Mom: Yes. Dad is going to drive us.

7   Trevor: Cool. I hope it'll be fun.

8   Mom: I sure hope so!

9   Amy: Mom, when are we going back to San Francisco?

10   Mom: In two weeks, Amy.

11   Amy: How long are we staying at Mt. Fuji?

12   Mom: Three days.

13   Trevor: Shouldn't we stay longer?

14   Mom: Three days should be good enough.

15   Trevor: Oh.

16   Amy: Where else are we going?

17   Mom: I don't think we have any more plans, so we'll be exploring a lot. You know, poking around malls, trying all sorts of food, stuff like that.

18	Amy:	Sounds good.
19	Mom:	I'm glad you like the plan. It would have been better if we had planned the trip out a little better.
20	Trevor:	It's fine. I'm already having a really good time even though we haven't done much.
21	Mom:	Good. Would you like to go have some sushi once Dad gets back?
22	Amy:	Yes! I'd love to try some sushi.
23	Mom:	You should like it. Everyone likes it.
24	Amy:	Really? I've heard that some people absolutely hate it.
25	Mom:	Don't worry.
26	Trevor:	Yeah. There is raw fish in it sometimes.
27	Amy:	Ew! I hate raw fish.
28	Mom:	Amy, chill out. You've never had it before. Well, here comes Dad.
29	Dad:	How are you guys?
30	Mom:	Good.
31	Trevor:	Awesome. Summer's going great.
32	Amy:	I don't think I'll like sushi.
33	Dad:	Why not?
34	Amy:	Raw fish.
35	Dad:	You've never even tried it!
36	Amy:	It sounds gross!
37	Dad:	Relax! Have you ever heard the saying "don't judge a book by its cover"? Do you remember the first time you tried crabmeat? You thought it was going to be gross but now it's one of your favorite foods.
38	Amy:	Yeah, but miracles don't happen twice.
39	Dad:	Sure they can. Just wait and see.

40	Trevor:	Yeah. Once you try sushi, we'll find out if you like it or not.
41	Mom:	Anyway, try it first and then judge.
42	Amy:	You guys are scaring me.
43	Mom:	We're teasing you because you are making fun of our favorite dish!
44	Amy:	I'm just saying!
45	Mom:	Maybe…but you've never tried it.
46	Amy:	So?
47	Mom:	Honey, just give it a try.
48	Dad:	(In the car) So, Amy, are you ready to try raw fish?
49	Amy:	Yeah. Don't blame me if I throw up.
50	Mom:	We won't.
51	Amy:	Good!
52	Trevor:	I'm blaming it on you.
53	Amy:	That's not nice.
54	Trevor:	It's not nice to throw up in restaurants.
55	Dad:	Stop bickering. It's time for you guys to grow up. Trevor, you are fourteen, and Amy, you are ten.
56	Trevor:	WE KNOW, DAD!
57	Dad:	Hey. No need to scream.
58	Mom:	Yeah. When we get back, we're going to teach you some manners.
59	Trevor:	Whatever.
60	Mom:	Trevor, this is not a 'whatever' situation. Also, who talks back to their parents like that?
61	Trevor:	Sorry, Mom.
62	Dad:	Okay, let's all lighten up. For heaven's sake, we're in Japan! We've been planning this for a year, and it's no good fighting the whole time.
63	Mom:	I suppose.

64	Dad:	We're here.
65	Dad:	(At the restaurant) Okay, Amy. Let's order some sushi.
66	Amy:	I'm ready.
67	Trevor:	This is going to be funny.
68	Mom:	I agree.
69	Dad:	(after sushi is served) Ready, set, go!
70	Amy:	Okay, here I go (Amy eats it)!
71	Mom:	How is it?
72	Amy:	Great. I love it.
73	Trevor:	Wow. I thought she would hate it.
74	Dad:	I told you miracles can happen twice.
75	Amy:	I guess so.

SKIT 8

AFTER SCHOOL ACTIVITY

2   Cody: (At school) Hey, Jack.

3   Jack: What?

4   Cody: You have plans after school?

5   Jack: No. Why?

6   Cody: Do you want to go see a movie?

7   Jack: Sure. What time?

8   Cody: We'll look it up soon.

9   Dylan: Hey, count me in.

10 Cody: Cool. Can you go?

11 Dylan: I think so.

12 Cody: Okay. I'll be right back. I'm going to go check the movie showtimes.

13 Jack: Okay. Make it fast.

14 Cody: Alright.

15 Cody: (after Cody checks) Alright. We have to walk there, which will take us about 15 minutes. It's three forty five (3:45) right now. There is one at four ten (4:10).

16 Dylan: Cool. Let's get going.

17 Cody: (At the AMC Theater) I'd like three tickets for the four ten (4:10) showing of Transformers.

18	Tim:	(ticket booth manager) Sure. That will be twenty seven dollars.
19	Cody:	Here you go. (to Tim and Dylan) Okay, you guys both owe me nine dollars.
20	Jack:	Sure thing.
21	Dylan:	I'll get it to you by tomorrow.
22	Cody:	Great. Do you guys want some popcorn or anything? It's on me.
23	Dylan:	Get me a Coke.
24	Jack:	I'm good.
25	Cody:	Okay. I'll go get a medium popcorn for three of us to share.
26	Tiffany:	(At the cashier) Is that all for you?
27	Cody:	Yes. A Coke and a medium popcorn.
28	Tiffany:	That'll come to eight forty nine ($8.49).
29	Cody:	Here you go.
30	Tiffany:	Enjoy your movie.
31	Cody:	Thank you.
32	Cody:	(After Cody buys the food) Okay, we still have five minutes until the movie starts. Do you guys want to go watch the trailers or do you guys want to go screw around for a bit?
33	Jack:	I like watching trailers. Let's go relax.
34	Dylan:	I'm with Jack.
35	Cody:	Yeah, that's what I was thinking, too.
36	Jack:	(After the movie) That was awesome.
37	Dylan:	Yeah, it was.
38	Cody:	I thought it was pretty good, too. Well, I called my mom, and she said that she'll pick us up and your parents can pick you guys up at my house.
39	Dylan:	Sounds great.

40	Jack:	Yeah. I've got to tell my brothers about this movie.
41	Mom:	(Getting picked up) So, did you guys have a lot of fun?
42	Dylan:	I don't know about them, but I had a spectacular time.
43	Cody:	So did I.
44	Jack:	Me too.
45	Mom:	Ok. I told your moms to come over to our house at seven (7:00).
46	Cody:	(At home) So, what do you guys want to do now?
47	Dylan:	Well, it's your house, Cody. You probably know what's fun and what's not. I mean, we can go play soccer or something, but it's up to you.
48	Cody:	Okay. Do you guys want to go on the tramp?
49	Jack:	The what?
50	Cody:	The tramp. Short for trampoline.
51	Jack:	You have one?
52	Cody:	Yeah.
53	Dylan:	What are we waiting for? Let's go!
54	Mom:	(7:00 PM) Come on in guys. It's almost seven. Your parents should be here any minute.
55	Cody:	Okay, Mom. We'll be right in.
56	Mom:	Keep your promise.
57	Cody:	Don't worry. Okay. Let's head inside in a minute.
58	Jack:	Okay. Well, we sure did have a lot of fun this afternoon.
59	Dylan:	I agree.
60	Cody:	Definitely.
61	Mom:	Jack!
62	Jack:	Yes?
63	Mom:	Your mom is here.

64 Cody: Okay, guys, let's go in now.

65 Cody: (After Cody's friends are gone) Hey, Mom, you should see the movie I saw today.

66 Mom: Why? Was it good?

67 Cody: Yes, excellent.

68 Mom: Alright, maybe sometime with your dad. Thanks for telling me.

69 Cody: Yeah, no problem.

70 Mom: Cody, why don't you go wash up?

71 Cody: Ok.

72 Mom: Good. Oh, by the way, Cody, I'm going to restrict you from hanging out after school from now on.

73 Cody: Why?

74 Mom: I looked through your grades and some of them don't look too great. I think you need to spend more time studying and reading rather than playing.

75 Cody: Let's make a deal. Every time I get an A on a test, I get to hang out after school.

76 Mom: Deal. I just want to see you work a little harder.

77 Cody: Got it.

Skit 9

BIKE RIDING WITH FRIENDS

2	Amber:	Watch out, because I'm pretty sure I'm going to crash.
3	Belinda:	That's fine. None of us are good at riding bikes.
4	Celia:	I think I'm getting the hang of it, though.
5	Deandra:	Me too. I like biking. I just hope I don't fall in the water!
6	Edmond:	Biking is lame. Skateboarding is where it's at.
7	Deandra:	Skateboarding is lame! You just swing your leg back and forth.
8	Edmond:	That's why it's fun!
9	Amber:	Really?
10	Edmond:	Yeah.
11	Belinda:	Okay, I'm going to the trail.
12	Celia:	Me too.
13	Deandra:	Me three!
14	Amber:	What? Me three?
15	Deandra:	Well, Celia said 'me too', so it's 'me three', and you should say 'me four'. It's a joke.
16	Amber:	Oh, I see. Me four!
17	Edmond:	That's goofy.

18	Amber:	Who cares.
19	Edmond:	You do.
20	Deandra:	Don't argue, guys.
21	Amber:	It was just for fun! I'm going to the trail. No more of the me too, me three thing.
22	Deandra:	Are you going, Edmond?
23	Belinda:	I hope not.
24	Edmond:	I'm going to my own trail.
25	Celia:	Yay!
26	Amber:	See ya! (I) Hope you don't die on your own trail!
27	Edmond:	Why would I die?
28	Belinda:	Your trail might be too hard for you!
29	Deandra:	Yeah, right.
30	Edmond:	What makes you think it's too hard?
31	Amber:	You just started skateboarding.
32	Celia:	Yeah.
33	Amber:	And we just got our bikes!
34	Edmond:	I'm going!
35	Belinda:	Okay, I'm going to crash.
36	Deandra:	Just try not to crash into people.
37	Belinda:	I don't try to!
38	Amber:	Just don't fall in the water. Go first, Belinda.
39	Celia:	I'm worried about this.
40	Deandra:	Why?
41	Celia:	Because I'm probably going to crash, too.
42	Amber:	Let's just go!
43	Deandra:	Come on! We only have thirty minutes left!
44	Belinda:	(screams) AAAHHHHHHH!!!
45	Deandra:	Are you okay?!
46	Belinda:	Yeah, I just crashed.
47	Amber:	Where?

48	Belinda:	Where? Do you mean what did I crash into?
49	Amber:	Yes, that's exactly what I mean.
50	Celia:	So, what did you crash into?
51	Belinda:	The bush with thorns.
52	Deandra:	That must've hurt.
53	Belinda:	Hurt? It burns!
54	Amber:	Let's see where you got hurt.
55	Belinda:	Everywhere.
56	Amber:	Ok, Deandra, would you go get the big first aid kit in my bike bag?
57	Deandra:	Sure.
58	Celia:	Belinda, you didn't hurt yourself everywhere.
59	Belinda:	That's what it feels like.
60	Amber:	Oh dear, look at that gash!
61	Belinda:	Eww.
62	Deandra:	Here's the first aid kit.
63	Amber:	Could you get a Band-Aid for her knee? A big one?
64	Deandra:	Yeah, here you go.
65	Celia:	And a small or medium one for her elbows.
66	Deandra:	That's good. The other ones are just scratches.
67	Belinda:	Okay, thanks.
68	Amber:	I'll stay with Belinda. You guys go ride your bikes.
69	Celia:	You sure?
70	Amber:	Yes, I'm getting tired anyway.
71	Deandra:	Okay. Here's your bike.
72	Edmond:	I just came back from my trail.
73	Amber:	Well, Belinda fell, and I'm staying with her.
74	Edmond:	I see that. Where are the others?
75	Amber:	On the trail.

76	Belinda:	I have a nasty one on my knee and we had to use a big Band-Aid for it.
77	Edmond:	Very pleasant.
78	Belinda:	It's not pleasant, it's gross.
79	Amber:	You should catch up with the others.
80	Edmond:	I will.

SKIT 10

BIRTHDAY PARTY

2	Isabel:	Mom, my birthday is in one month! Shouldn't we start planning the party?
3	Mom:	I think we can wait a little. Let's talk about this later, when we are on our way home from dinner.
4	Daniel:	Yeah, seriously. Just enjoy the dinner.
5	Dad:	He's right! We don't get to eat out at a place like this everyday!
6	Note:	(After Dinner)
7	Isabel:	Now can we plan my birthday party?
8	Daniel:	Not when I'm here.
9	Mom:	Why not?
10	Daniel:	I don't want to hear about it.
11	Dad:	That was a wonderful dinner, wasn't it?
12	Isabel:	Mom, let's get planning!
13	Mom:	What do you want to do?
14	Dad:	We've got to have food.
15	Mom:	Obviously.
16	Isabel:	Balloons too!
17	Daniel:	Helium filled?
18	Mom:	Yes, of course.
19	Isabel:	We also need a cake!

20	Daniel:	That's considered food.
21	Mom:	A piñata!
22	Dad:	I think we better have a theme!
23	Isabel:	Yes! That's a great idea!
24	Mom:	What's your theme going to be?
25	Daniel:	I bet you want to do something with Barbies!
26	Isabel:	Hey! That's not true!
27	Mom:	Don't be mean, Daniel.
28	Isabel:	It's going to be puppies!
29	Dad:	Small ones?
30	Isabel:	Yes! The white cuddly ones!
31	Mom:	I think they might be like Maltese Poodles
32	Note:	(At Home)
33	Daniel:	I'm going to look up Maltese Poodle images on Google.
34	Isabel:	That's a great idea. I think this is the first time we agreed on something, right?
35	Note:	(Daniel is silent...)
36	Isabel:	Answer me, or I will answer myself! True.
37	Dad:	Are we getting all the stuff for your party tomorrow?
38	Isabel:	Why not? Sounds like a great idea to me!
39	Mom:	Oh my gosh! We need to have goody bags! I totally forgot!
40	Dad:	I forgot, too. Isabel, how about you?
41	Isabel:	I didn't think about that.
42	Daniel:	I found them! They are so cute!
43	Isabel:	I want one!
44	Mom:	Of course, you can have one, Isabel!
45	Note:	(Next Day)
46	Isabel:	We are going to Target, right?

47	Dad:	Why?
48	Isabel:	They have the best stuff!
49	Dad:	Sure, why not?
50	Note:	(In Target)
51	Tim:	How may I help you?
52	Dad:	We are buying things for this young lady's birthday party.
53	Tim:	Wonderful. I will lead you to our party section.
54	Dad:	This is perfect, thank you.
55	Note:	(At the party section)
56	Dad:	These are perfect for the goody bags, aren't they?
57	Isabel:	Yes, they look good to me.
58	Dad:	Alright.
59	Isabel:	Look at that piñata! It's perfect! It looks like a Maltese Poodle!
60	Dad:	Okay, is that it? I think we got everything.
61	Note:	(At home)
62	Mom:	Look at the piñata! It's perfect!
63	Daniel:	It's okay.
64	Note:	(2 weeks from the birthday party)
65	Isabel:	I will give an invitation to Betty and Kyla.
66	Mom:	That's it?
67	Isabel:	No.
68	Dad:	Who else?
69	Isabel:	Rebecca and Sarah.
70	Note:	(Party Day)
71	Isabel:	(opens the door for Rebecca and Kyla) Hi.
72	Rebecca:	Hi, Isabel. Congrats!
73	Kyla:	Hi, Isabel. Happy birthday!
74	Isabel:	Okay, we're going to wait for Betty and Sarah.
75	Rebecca:	Okay.

76	Kyla:	Sounds good.
77	Note:	(Doorbell rings)
78	Isabel:	Hi, Betty! Hi, Sarah!
79	Betty:	Hey! Happy birthday!
80	Kyla:	Hi, Betty!
81	Sarah:	Isabel! Aww, happy birthday!
82	Isabel:	Alright, let's start playing some games. We have limbo set up.
83	Betty:	Where should we put your presents?
84	Isabel:	I totally forgot about the presents! I will ask my mom.
85	Isabel:	Mom, where should they put the presents?
86	Mom:	On the table is fine.
87	Note:	(Back to friends)
88	Isabel:	She said on the table is fine.
89	Kyla:	Okay.
90	Note:	(Playing Limbo)
91	Betty:	I think my back is going to break soon.
92	Isabel:	Don't say that!
93	Betty:	I was just joking!
94	Kyla:	Good!
95	Sarah:	I can't wait until the dance!
96	Isabel:	How did you know we were having a dance?
97	Sarah:	It was just a good guess.
98	Kyla:	Cool! I love dancing!
99	Isabel:	Great. We will have more kids joining us later.
100	Elizabeth:	Like who?
101	Jessica:	Any boys?
102	Isabel:	Nope. Katelyn, Candace, and Brittney are coming.
103	Jessica:	Not a bad group.

104	Note:	(Bobbing for Apples)
105	Betty:	My mouth is not big!
106	Sarah:	Mine isn't either!
107	Kyla:	This is exciting!
108	Sarah:	I hate being small!
109	Betty:	Don't worry. You'll grow. You had the advantage when we played limbo, though.
110	Rebecca:	Yeah, you won!
111	Kyla:	I wish the apples were smaller!
112	Rebecca:	It would be easier if they were.
113	Isabel:	Yeah. I'm next.
114	Betty:	This is fun!
115	Note:	(A contest to eat donuts hanging from a fan)
116	Isabel:	Dad, could you turn on the fan on the slowest mode?
117	Dad:	Sure.
118	Rebecca:	I should've worn better shoes!
119	Isabel:	I wonder why people aren't showing up yet.
120	Betty:	Yeah.
121	Note:	(Doorbell rings)
122	Rebecca:	Here they are!
123	Brittney:	Hi, birthday girl!!
124	Candace:	Happy birthday, Isabel.
125	Katelyn:	Hi!
126	Isabel:	Hi, guys! We've been waiting for you guys. Come on, let's go dance!
127	Note:	(At the dance party)
128	Katelyn:	Turn up the music!
129	Sarah:	Is there anything to eat?
130	Isabel:	Yeah! It's upstairs!
131	Betty:	I'm getting tired.

132 Sarah: Take a break.

133 Kyla: There is one thing we need, a rave playlist.

134 Isabel: I forgot! I have one.

135 Betty: You should totally get it out.

136 Rebecca: This is what I call a rave!

137 Brittney: I'm going to go get some food!

138 Note: (Back Upstairs)

139 Katelyn: I didn't notice I was so hungry!

140 Kyla: I know! The dance was so fun I didn't even think about food.

141 Candace: Did you plan anything else?

142 Isabel: Are you kidding me? Of course I did! How can you forget the piñata and the cake?

143 Kyla: Let's go beat up the piñata!

144 Note: (Kids hit the piñata taking turns)

145 Candace: My turn. Ah! I almost broke it!

146 Brittney: Ready, aim, hit! Oh my gosh, I broke it!

147 Sarah: What are you guys doing standing there? Pick the candy up!

148 Kyla: Sorry! I didn't realize you broke it!

149 Brittney: Talk about stupid.

150 Kyla: Hey! That's not nice!

151 Candace: I picked up so much!

152 Note: (Inside after picking up all the candy)

153 Kyla: I picked up forty nine! Sarah! How many did you get?

154 Isabel: Fifty four! I beat you!

155 Katelyn: Thirty seven for me!

156 Brittney: Sixty four!

157 Sarah:

158 Candace: Forty nine!

159	Betty:	Sixty nine!!
160	Isabel:	And the winner is, (drumroll) BETTY!
161	Betty:	Whoo!
162	Candace:	Congrats!
163	Sarah:	Congratulations!
164	Kyla:	Yeah, congrats!
165	Betty:	(like a star does to his/her fans) Thank you! Thank you! Thank you!
166	Sarah:	This isn't a show, Betty.
167	Katelyn:	She's pretending.
168	Candace:	Wait, my mom is calling.
169	Note:	(Candace comes back)
170	Candace:	My mom is coming in fifteen minutes to pick me up.
171	Isabel:	Hurry! Get the cake and presents!
172	Note:	(Eyeryone sings "Happy birthday".)
173	Betty:	I want a slice!
174	Sarah:	Everyone does!
175	Note:	(Presents)
176	Isabel:	That is so nice of you Brittney!
177	Brittney:	I'm glad that you like it.
178	Isabel:	Candace, how did you know I wanted this?
179	Candace:	Because I wanted it!
180	Isabel:	Well, since your birthday is next week, I will get you one.
181	Candace:	No need to. My mom bought two! One for you, and one for me.
182	Note:	(Car pulls up)
183	Elizabeth:	That would be Candace's mom.
184	Isabel:	Aww, I wish you could stay longer, Candace.
185	Jessica:	Me too!

186 Rebecca: I wish this party was a sleep over!

187 Betty: I think my mom is here, too.

188 Isabel: Thanks for coming to my birthday party!

189 Candace: Bye! Happy birthday again!

190 Isabel: Bye!

SKIT 11

A TYPICAL DAY OF LIFE

2	Mom:	(Part 1) Wake up, sleepyhead. It's time to get up. Your alarm has been going off for ten minutes!
3	Sarah:	I don't want to go to school! I'm too tired.
4	Mom:	Well, you shouldn't have stayed up so late reading in bed.
5	Sarah:	I know but I was reading this amazing book about how your body works, and it had really cool pictures of the skeletons and muscles.
6	Mom:	That sounds very interesting, but your body really needs more rest. That way, it won't be so hard to get up in the morning.
7	Sarah:	Is Steven up yet?
8	Mom:	No, I'm going to wake him up now. Start picking out some clothes to wear.
9	Sarah:	What's the weather going to be like today?
10	Mom:	It's going to be pretty sunny, but cloudy and cool in the morning.
11	Mom:	If you want to wear a dress, you should probably wear tights and a sweater.

12	Sarah:	Thanks, Mom. Can I wear my shiny black shoes, too?
13	Mom:	I don't think that would be a good idea. You have gym today and need running shoes. Besides, you'll only get them dirty at recess.
14	Sarah:	I guess you're right. And I want to run up and down the hill on the playground.
15	Mom:	Okay, sweetie, get yourself ready and I'm going to get Steven going.
16	Steven:	I'm up, Mom, but I don't feel well. I don't think I can go to school today.
17	Mom:	What's bothering you?
18	Steven:	My stomach and head hurt.
19	Mom:	Let me feel your forehead. Yeah, it does seem a little warm. Why don't you get up and have some toast? We'll see how you feel after that.
20	Steven:	But I don't want to go school. I want to stay home with you!
21	Mom:	I know you do, but if you feel well enough, you really need to be at school. Think about how much you will miss your friends.
22	Sarah:	Mom! I can't find my pink tights. Have you seen them?
23	Mom:	Sarah, please don't yell. Have you checked the laundry room? I just washed a bunch of things so they might be hanging in there.
24	Sarah:	I already looked in there.
25	Mom:	Did you check your closet?
26	Sarah:	Yes, of course I did.

27	Mom:	They are probably still in the hamper then. Just wear your brown ones. They'll look cute with the orange and red in your dress.
28	Sarah:	Okay, fine. But I really want my pink ones.
29	Steven:	Mom, I really don't feel well.
30	Mom:	Do you want to try eating some toast? Sometimes your body just needs a little energy to get going in the morning.
31	Steven:	I don't want anything.
32	Mom:	Do you feel like you are going to throw up? Okay, why don't you lay down on the couch and rest?
33	Steven:	No, my stomach just really hurts.
34	Mom:	Have you tried going to the bathroom?
35	Steven:	I don't need to. Oh, wait, I do.
36	Mom:	Sarah, what would you like for breakfast?
37	Sarah:	I want pancakes with syrup and chocolate chips.
38	Mom:	Sweetie, we only have those kinds of pancakes on the weekends.
39	Sarah:	What days are the weekend?
40	Mom:	Saturday and Sunday. Today is Wednesday, and there just isn't enough time to make pancakes.
41	Sarah:	Well, can't Daddy make them?
42	Mom:	No, Honey. Daddy has to get ready for work.
43	Sarah:	Okay, I guess I'll have a bagel.
44	Mom:	Do you want it with butter or cream cheese?
45	Sarah:	I'll have it with butter. Can I have some orange juice, too?
46	Mom:	Sure, Honey.

47	Steven:	Mom, I went to the bathroom and I still feel sick.
48	Mom:	I'm sorry you don't feel well, Honey. Let's take your temperature.
49	Steven:	Are you going to use the humidifier?
50	Sarah:	Steven, don't be dumb. It's called a thermometer.
51	Mom:	Sarah, it is not okay to talk to your brother that way and use those kinds of words. He is only four and doesn't always remember the names of everything like you do.
52	Sarah:	Sorry.
53	Mom:	Tell Steven, not me.
54	Note:	(Sarah walks over and gives Steven a hug.)
55	Sarah:	Sorry, bro.
56	Steven:	It's ok.
57	Dad:	Good morning, everyone. How are my kids doing today?
58	Sarah:	I'm great, Daddy, but Steven isn't feeling well.
59	Dad:	What's wrong, little monkey?
60	Steven:	I feel hot and then cold and my stomach hurts.
61	Dad:	Did you take his temperature?
62	Mom:	I was just about to. Okay, hold still, Honey. Uh oh, it looks like you have a fever.
63	Dad:	How high is it?
64	Mom:	It's at one oh one (101). I guess you'll have to stay home after all.
65	Dad:	What are you going to do about work?
66	Mom:	I only have one client today, so I can work from home.

67	Dad:	Are you sure? I can try to reschedule my day if you need me to.
68	Mom:	No, that's ok. November seems to be a slow month for me anyway. Can you take Sarah to school?
69	Dad:	Sure. Do you need me to pick up anything at the store on my way home?
70	Mom:	That would be great.
71	Dad:	What do you want me to get?
72	Mom:	Here's the list, but let me think because there are a few more things that we need. Let me see, we have milk and eggs, but we need bread.
73	Dad:	Why don't you go look in the refrigerator and tell me what we need. I'll make the list.
74	Mom:	Okay. Go ahead and put down lettuce and carrots.
75	Steven:	Don't forget ice cream!
76	Mom:	I don't think you'll be eating any ice cream anytime soon. Maybe we should have Daddy pick up some Jell-O and crackers, though.
77	Sarah:	Can you get some pears, Daddy? They're my favorite fruit and I'm tired of eating only apples.
78	Dad:	Sure, sweetheart.
79	Sarah:	Also, I want to start bringing small juice boxes in my lunch.
80	Dad:	What's wrong with your Thermos?
81	Sarah:	It keeps leaking and the other kids have juice boxes. Yesterday, my whole lunch got wet and soggy. It was gross.

82	Dad:	Alright, I'll find something for you to drink.
83	Mom:	Sarah, come to the table. Your breakfast is ready. Here, your gummy vitamins too.
84	Sarah:	Thanks, Mom.
85	Mom:	You are very welcome. Any requests for your lunch today?
86	Sarah:	Could I have a peanut butter and, Honey sandwich?
87	Mom:	We are all out of, Honey. Is jelly ok?
88	Sarah:	Sure. Dad, guess you'd better add, Honey to the list. Get the cute kind in the bottle that looks like a bear.
89	Dad:	Got it.
90	Mom:	Hurry up and eat, Sarah. We still need to brush your hair and you don't want to be late.
91	Sarah:	What time is it?
92	Mom:	Half past seven (7:30). You and Daddy need to leave in ten minutes.
93	Sarah:	Can you just brush my hair while I'm eating, please?
94	Mom:	Okay, I don't see why not. Actually, I think I need to spray it with some water and then some detangling spray. It's pretty messy.
95	Dad:	You must have had some wild dreams last night.
96	Sarah:	Actually, I had this wonderful dream where Steven and I were riding horses and then they grew wings and we were flying all over the city.
97	Mom:	That sounds like a great dream!
98	Steven:	What color was my horse, Sarah?

99	Sarah:	It was white, but it had a purple mane and a pink tail.
100	Steven:	That sounds so pretty!
101	Sarah:	My horse was black with rainbow colored hair.
102	Steven:	I don't ever remember any of my dreams.
103	Sarah:	Ouch, Mom. You're brushing it too hard.
104	Mom:	Hold still, there are a lot of knots in there.
105	Dad:	When you are done with breakfast, run upstairs and brush your teeth.
106	Sarah:	Okay, Daddy. I can't wait to ride with you to school.
107	Mom:	Come on, let's get moving. Stop playing around and finish up.
108	Sarah:	I'm all done.
109	Mom:	Please put your dishes in the sink.
110	Steven:	Mom, can I have some water?
111	Mom:	Sure. Let me put it into a cup with a straw so you don't spill on the couch.
112	Dad:	Do you think a doctor needs to see him?
113	Mom:	I'm not sure. I'll wait and see how the day goes.
114	Dad:	I hope he doesn't have the flu.
115	Mom:	I've heard there is a flu going around, but hopefully it is just a cold.
116	Dad:	Okay, Sarah, let's go brush your teeth.
117	Sarah:	Can I put the toothpaste on? I want the blue sparkly kind, not the green spicy one.
118	Dad:	That's fine. But squeeze the tube slowly so it doesn't come out all at once.
119	Sarah:	I can't get the cap off. Can you help me?

120	Dad:	Here you go.
121	Sarah:	Thanks, Daddy.
122	Dad:	Okay, which shoes do you want to wear?
123	Sarah:	I think I should wear my running shoes, but these boots would look really cute, too.
124	Dad:	Did I hear Mom say that you have gym today?
125	Sarah:	Oh, I forgot. I guess I shouldn't wear boots.
126	Dad:	Can you tie them or do you need help?
127	Sarah:	I think I can tie them. First make two bunny ears, right?
128	Dad:	That's right. Then one bunny goes around the other and through the hole.
129	Sarah:	Can you double knot them for me? I can't get the laces as tight as you can.
130	Dad:	Sure. Ready to go now?
131	Sarah:	I just need to get my backpack and put on my coat.
132	Mom:	You might want to put on a hat and gloves, too. It's actually quite chilly out now.
133	Sarah:	Okay, but I think I left them at Lexy's house.
134	Steven:	You can borrow mine. I'm staying in my jammies today, right, Mom?
135	Mom:	That's right, Honey. That was really nice of you to offer to share your hat and gloves with your sister, but I think they may be too small for her.
136	Sarah:	Yeah, shrimp. You're only four.
137	Steven:	But I'm going to be five soon.
138	Sarah:	True, but you're still little.

139	Mom:	I think we have another pair you can use. Make sure you get your gloves back from Lexy today when you go to her house.
140	Sarah:	I'm going over to her house? I'm so excited!
141	Mom:	Okay, you can cheer later. Go get your backpack.
142	Sarah:	Uh oh.
143	Mom:	What's wrong?
144	Sarah:	I think I forgot to do my homework.
145	Mom:	Sarah, this is not okay. You told me that you didn't have homework yesterday.
146	Sarah:	I know, I'm just kidding! I don't have any homework, but today is 'show and tell'. Can I bring my Strawberry Shortcake doll in?
147	Mom:	That's fine. Just make sure you don't lose her hat.
148	Sarah:	I won't. We have to keep our toys in our backpacks all day anyway.
149	Steven:	Am I missing 'show and tell' at my school?
150	Mom:	No, your 'show and tell' day is Friday.
151	Steven:	Oh good. I don't like being sick on those days.
152	Mom:	Well, if you rest a lot today, hopefully you will be able to go back to school by Friday.
153	Dad:	I'm going to go warm up the car. Sarah, come on out when you are all packed up.
154	Sarah:	Okay. I'm almost ready.
155	Mom:	Here is your lunch.
156	Sarah:	Did you pack cheese puffs?
157	Mom:	Yes, I did.
158	Sarah:	Carrots?

159	Mom:	No, I had to throw those away. They were mushy.
160	Sarah:	Dad, put carrots on the shopping list!
161	Mom:	Thanks, Honey, but I don't think he can hear you. He's in the garage.
162	Sarah:	Okay, I'll tell him when I get in the car.
163	Mom:	I appreciate that.
164	Sarah:	Did you put a special note in my lunch?
165	Mom:	You are just going to have to wait and see.
166	Sarah:	I love your notes, Mom. You draw the best hearts!
167	Mom:	I hope they make you smile during lunch.
168	Dad:	Let's get going, Sarah! Grab your backpack.
169	Sarah:	Okay, I'm coming. Bye, Mom.
170	Mom:	Have a good day, sweetie, I love you.
171	Sarah:	Thanks, Mom, I love you too. Bye Steven, hope you feel better!
172	Steven:	Thanks, Sarah. I will.
173	Dad:	(Sarah gets in the car with her dad.) Are you buckled up?
174	Sarah:	Almost, I can't reach the buckle part. It's stuck under my carseat.
175	Dad:	Do you need help?
176	Sarah:	No, I think I got it. Ok, I'm ready.
177	Dad:	Do you want to listen to some music?
178	Sarah:	Sure, did you bring the iPod?
179	Dad:	I did. Let's listen to your mix.
180	Sarah:	Okay! Are you picking me up?
181	Dad:	Nope, you're going to Lexy's house, remember?

182	Sarah:	Oh yeah, I forgot. Daddy, can you park in the school parking lot and walk me to my classroom?
183	Dad:	If we get there early enough.
184	Sarah:	Well, if there are too many cars, I guess you can just drop me off.
185	Dad:	Here we are. It looks like there aren't any parking spots, Honey. I'm sorry.
186	Sarah:	That's ok. I see Lexy. Bye, Dad.
187	Dad:	Bye, sweetie. Have a good day!
188	Sarah:	Hey, Lexy, what's going on?
189	Lexy:	Not much. I can't wait for you to come over today. I just got a new paint set and my mom said we can use it.
190	Sarah:	Cool, that sounds like fun.
191	Ashley	Hey Sarah, Lexy, want to go run up the hill with me?
192	Sarah:	Do we have time? I think the bell is going to ring soon.
193	Lexy:	Nah, let's just go. Our teacher never opens the door on time.
194	Sarah:	Last one to the top is a rotten egg.
195	Lexy:	(The girls run up and down and the bell rings) We made it back just in time.
196	Sarah:	Where is Mrs. Tyler?
197	Ashley	I don't know but she usually opens the door by now.
198	Lexy:	Ooh, look! We have a sub today.
199	Bryan:	Sweet. Now we can goof off all day.

200	Ashley:	Bryan, just because we have a sub doesn't mean we can play around. She might tell the teacher that we were behaving badly.
201	Bryan:	Well, you can do whatever you want. I'm going to have fun.
202	Note:	(The teacher opens the door and the kids walk in.)
203	Ms. Jansen:	Hello, boys and girls. Come on in and hang up your backpacks and coats. Mrs. Tyler is home sick today with a bad cold.
204	Sarah:	My little brother is sick, too. Why is everyone getting so sick all of a sudden?
205	Ms. Jansen:	It could be the big change in weather. Many people get sick when the weather suddenly gets cold.
206	Susie:	My mom says the bad weather doesn't make you get a cold.
207	Ms. Jansen:	It's not really the actual weather, but more that people are forced to be indoors more, so there is higher chance of germs spreading.
208	Susie:	That's why you have to wash your hands all the time, right?
209	Ms. Jansen:	That's right. It is always good to wash your hands with soap a lot during the day.
210	Bryan:	What about your feet? Should you wash those?
211	Seth:	Well, you should Bryan, because yours stink.
212	Ms. Jansen:	(The whole class giggles) Okay, boys and girls. That's enough. Settle down and find your seats.

213	Ms. Jansen:	As I mentioned before, Mrs. Tyler is home sick, but I expect all of you to be on your best behavior.
214	Ms. Jansen:	I will report to Mrs. Tyler anyone who messes around.
215	Ashley:	See, Bryan. I told you, you have to be good.
216	Bryan:	I can do whatever I want.
217	Susie:	Okay, Bryan, but you're going to just get in trouble and miss recess.
218	Sarah:	I don't think boys are very smart.
219	Lexy:	Same. Except my big brother. He's thirteen and he's really smart.
220	Ms. Jansen:	That's enough, everyone. Please take out your science journals and something to write with.
221	Sarah:	What are we doing today?
222	Ms. Jansen:	We are going to make some observations using all five of our senses. Can anyone tell me what an observation is?
223	Susie:	It's paying attention to something and watching it.
224	Ms. Jansen:	Very good, but did you know that looking or using your eyes is only one of the ways to make an observation?
225	Ms. Jansen:	Can someone tell me another way to make an observation?
226	Ms. Jansen:	(David raises his hand) Yes, David?
227	David	You can touch something with your hands.
228	Bryan:	Or your elbow.
229	Ms. Jansen:	Thank you, Bryan, but please raise your hand if you have something to add.
230	Ashley:	Can't you also smell something?

231	Ms. Jansen:	That's right. You can use your nose to observe how something smells.
232	Bryan:	Yeah, like my smelly feet.
233	Ms. Jansen:	Bryan, that's enough. If you shout out one more time, you are going to have to stay inside during recess.
234	Bryan:	You can't do that!
235	Ms. Jansen:	Yes, I can. I suggest that you cooperate and show some respect for your class.
236	Bryan:	Sorry.
237	Ms. Jansen:	Your apology is accepted. Please show us now that you can listen quietly and be a part of this discussion.
238	Ms. Jansen:	Let's continue. Tell me what else you can use.
239	Lexy:	What about your ears?
240	Ms. Jansen:	Yes, you can use your ears to hear things.
241	Sarah:	Oh, I know. You can taste something.
242	Ms. Jansen:	That is the fifth (5th) one. When tasting something, however, please make sure it's safe to put in your mouth.
243	Bryan:	I want to go taste my lunch now. Is it time to eat yet?
244	Ms. Jansen:	(The whole class giggles) That's it, Bryan. You just lost your recess.
245	Bryan:	Oh, man!
246	Ashley:	We told you to be good.
247	Ms. Jansen:	Okay, class. I would like you to make ten different observations around the classroom and write them down in your science journal.
248	Sarah:	Can we go outside to observe?

249	Ms. Jansen:	Let's have everyone stay inside because it looks like it's going to rain any second now.
250	Sarah:	Could I make an observation of the rain?
251	Ms. Jansen:	That's an excellent idea.
252	Lexy:	I like the way it smells when it rains.
253	Ms. Jansen:	That's a great observation, too.
254	Ms. Jansen:	(Twenty minutes go by as the kids write their observations) Boys and girls. We're going to take a few more minutes and finish up.
255	Sarah:	Is it time for lunch?
256	Ms. Jansen:	Just about. When you are done with your journal can you put it in your desk and line up for lunch?
257	Ashley	(During lunch hour) Hey, Lexy. What do you have for lunch?
258	Lexy:	I'm having hot lunch today because they're serving chicken enchiladas. They're my favorite.
259	Sarah:	I thought they were serving that on Thursday?
260	Lexy:	Oh, I forgot. I thought it was Thursday. What do they serve on Tuesdays?
261	Ashley:	It's not Tuesday, silly. It is Wednesday.
262	Lexy:	I keep forgetting what day it is.
263	Sarah:	Well, let's just hurry up and eat so we can go out to recess.
264	Ashley:	Does anybody want to trade something for my banana?
265	Sarah:	I thought you loved bananas.
266	Ashley:	I do, but only when they're yellow. This one has lots of brown spots.
267	Susie:	How about some grapes?

268	Ashley:	What color are they?
269	Susie:	Red.
270	Ashley:	Ok, let's trade! Thanks!
271	Lexy:	Come on. Let's finish so we can go play. I don't think it's raining anymore.
272	Susie:	Oh no, it's snowing!
273	Class	Snow!!!
274	Sarah:	Come on! Let's get outside before we have to stay inside.
275	Lexy:	I want to run back to the class and get my hat and gloves.
276	Sarah:	Good idea. I don't want my hands or head to get cold (The kids go outside and play in the snow)
277	Note:	(At home)
278	Mom:	Do you feel like eating anything?
279	Steven:	Can I have some juice? I'm a little thirsty.
280	Mom:	Sure. Why don't you have a few crackers too?
281	Steven:	Okay. Can I watch TV?
282	Mom:	What do you want to watch?
283	Steven:	I want to watch Sesame Street.
284	Mom:	Okay, I'll be right back with your juice and crackers.
285	Steven:	Mom, my stomach still hurts.
286	Mom:	Well, just rest on the couch and I'll put on your show.
287	Steven:	I like Big Bird. He sings the colors of the rainbow. (Singing) Red, and yellow and pink and green. Purple and orange and blue…
288	Mom:	Don't sing too loudly. I want you to take it easy.

289	Steven:	I hope the Cookie Monster is in this one. He's funny.
290	Mom:	What color is he again? Blue or green?
291	Steven:	Oh, Mom, you know he is blue.
292	Mom:	Let me feel your head again. My goodness, you're really hot again. Let's take your temperature.
293	Steven:	But I feel better, Mom.
294	Mom:	I know, but we should make sure. Oh no, your fever has gotten much higher. It's a hundred and three now (103).
295	Mom:	I think I'd better take you to the doctor and make sure you are okay.
296	Steven:	Am I going to have to get any shots? I don't like getting shots. They make my arm hurt.
297	Mom:	I don't think you will need a shot, but probably some medicine.
298	Steven:	I hope it's cherry flavored.
299	Mom:	You can keep your pajamas on, but I want you to wear a coat. It's cold outside.
300	Steven:	I thought you said it was going to be sunny today?
301	Mom:	Well, sometimes the weather forecast can be wrong.
302	Steven:	Can you carry me? I don't feel like walking.
303	Mom:	Of course.
304	Note:	(Part 2 - At the Doctor's office)
305	Nurse:	Hi, sweetie. What's your name?
306	Steven:	My name is Steven.
307	Nurse:	That's a good name! What's your last name?
308	Steven:	Bright.

309	Nurse:	I see, Mr. Steven Bright. How old are you?
310	Steven:	I'm four years old, but I'm going to turn five soon.
311	Nurse:	Really? I have a four year old daughter just like you!
312	Steven:	What school does she go to?
313	Nurse:	She goes to Boulder Valley Preschool.
314	Steven:	Really? I go to the same school! What's her name?
315	Nurse:	Her name is Tina, Tina Simpson.
316	Steven:	I know her. She is not in my class, but I see her often during recess.
317	Nurse:	Is that true? It's a small world, isn't it?
318	Steven:	Yeah, it is.
319	Nurse:	(looking at Steven's mom) So what's going on with Steven?
320	Mom:	He's had a fever all morning and it's getting worse. He says his stomach hurts too.
321	Nurse:	Has he eaten anything today?
322	Mom:	Not really. Just some juice and a few crackers.
323	Nurse:	Okay. Let's go see how much he weighs. Come over here, Steven, and step on the scale.
324	Steven:	Is it going to hurt?
325	Nurse:	No, sweetie. You just stand there while I move these squares.
326	Mom:	How much does he weigh?
327	Nurse:	Almost 40 pounds.
328	Mom:	Wow, Steven, you've gained weight since last month. You were thirty eight pounds then.
329	Nurse:	Okay, follow me back to the room and I'll take your blood pressure and temperature.

330	Steven:	Is that going to hurt?
331	Nurse:	Nope. It will just feel like your arm is getting a big hug.
332	Steven:	Oh, you're right. This just feels funny.
333	Nurse:	Your blood pressure looks just fine.
334	Steven:	That's weird. How can it be normal when my stomach really hurts so much?
335	Mom:	Steven, it just means your stomachache is not so bad.
336	Nurse:	Now let me take your temperature.
337	Steven:	Mom took it already this morning, and she said I had a fever.
338	Nurse:	She did? But your body temperature can change over time especially when you are sick. Sweetie, hold still for me.
339	Steven:	I still have a fever, don't I?
340	Nurse:	Yes, I can see that. The doctor will be here in just a minute.
341	Mom:	Okay. Thanks.
342	Nurse:	No problem. I hope you feel better soon, Steven.
343	Steven:	Thanks.
344	Doctor:	(Knocking) Hi, Steven, how are you today?
345	Steven:	Not too well. I feel really gross.
346	Doctor:	Well, let's take a look and see what's going on. I'm going to look in your ears and mouth. Alright, your ears look fine. Say ahhhhhhhh. Hmmm, your throat is a little swollen. Does it hurt to swallow?
347	Steven:	No, not really.

348	Doctor:	Now I'm going to feel your neck and then listen to your heartbeat. Take a few deep breaths for me.
349	Mom:	Do you think he has the flu?
350	Doctor:	It's hard to tell, but it's possible. Has he had a runny nose or a cough?
351	Mom:	No, mostly just a fever and he has been complaining about his stomach hurting.
352	Doctor:	Well, your heart and lungs sound fine. (to mom) I would say just take some Children's Tylenol for fever and get lots of rest. Make sure he drinks plenty of fluids.
353	Mom:	Thanks, doctor.
354	Doctor:	You're welcome. If he isn't better in the next two to three days, give us a call.
355	Steven:	Can I go pick out a sticker?
356	Doctor:	Of course you may!
357	Steven:	I want to get a tiger sticker. Can I get one for my sister, too?
358	Doctor:	Of course. That is really nice of you to think of your sister.
359	Mom:	Get your shoes on and let's go.
360	Steven:	Can you help me with my socks? I can't get them on.
361	Mom:	Here you go. I'll help you with your shoes too.
362	Steven:	Thanks, Mom, but I want to do those myself.
363	Mom:	Okay. I know you are a big boy and can do it yourself.
364	Note:	(Back at school)
365	Lexy:	I got my socks all wet.

366	Sarah:	That's because you didn't bring any boots to school.
367	Lexy:	I know. I just wanted to wear my fancy shoes. They look so cute with this dress, but I guess they aren't the best for the playground.
368	Sarah:	They do look nice.
369	Ms. Jansen:	Class, please get out your reading books and writing journals.
370	Ms. Jansen:	I'm going to meet with reading groups and while I'm doing that, I would like the rest of you to write a story.
371	Ashley:	What should we write about?
372	Ms. Jansen:	Why don't you write a story about something silly that has happened to you before.
373	Sarah:	That sounds like fun!
374	Ms. Jansen:	I'm going to meet with the green group first.
375	Sarah:	That's my group. Oh well, I guess I can write later.
376	Ms. Jansen:	Okay. Green group, what book are you reading?
377	Sarah:	We are reading "Fox on Wheels".
378	Ms. Jansen:	Who can tell me the main character?
379	Joe:	That's easy, it's Fox.
380	Ms. Jansen:	And who can tell me why Fox isn't very happy?
381	Sarah:	Because he has to babysit his little sister.
382	Ms. Jansen:	Why does that make him upset?
383	Susie:	He would rather be playing at the park and riding bikes with his friends.
384	Ms. Jansen:	Good. Sarah, why don't you start reading chapter two for us?

385	Sarah:	"Fox scowled at his little sister. He wanted to be with his friends and all she wanted to do was play dolls."
386	Ms. Jansen:	Joe, please continue.
387	Joe:	"Fox thought that maybe if he found something to keep his sister busy, he could just leave her alone for a few minutes."
388	Ms. Jansen:	Good job, Joe. Susie, would you please continue?
389	Susie:	Okay. "Fox gave his sister one of his favorite toys. "Here, little sister," he said."
390	Susie:	"You stay here and play with this, but you can't leave this spot. Okay?"
391	Ms. Jansen:	Let's stop there. Do you think this is a good idea?
392	Green Group	No!
393	Ms. Jansen:	What do you think might happen?
394	Sarah:	I think if Fox leaves his sister alone, he is going to get in trouble.
395	Susie:	I think his little sister is too little to be alone. She could get hurt.
396	Ms. Jansen:	You are both probably right. Sometimes we have to do things we don't want to do. Great job reading!
397	Ms. Jansen:	Your homework for tonight is to read to page ten. When you get back to your desks, you can start writing your story.
398	Note:	(Some time passes and the kids are working on their stories.)

399	Ms. Jansen:	Everyone, please start to wrap up your stories because class ends in five minutes!
400	Lexy:	(The class cheers) Hi, Sarah, you know, you will come over to my house after school, right?
401	Sarah:	After soccer practice.
402	Lexy:	Oh, yeah, I forgot. I have soccer practice.
403	Sarah:	Silly, we're on the same team.
404	Lexy:	I don't know why I forgot about that.
405	Sarah:	We can hang out after practice.
406	Ms. Jansen:	Boys and girls, please finish up your stories and put away your journals.
407	Ms. Jansen:	Once you have done that, you may put your things away and get ready to go home.
408	Sarah:	Come on, we can walk out together.
409	Mom:	(The bell rings and the kids all run outside) Hi, Sarah. How was school?
410	Sarah:	Pretty good, we had a substitute teacher today and Bryan was really rude to her.
411	Mom:	Oh, how disappointing.
412	Sarah:	She was a really nice teacher, but he got in trouble.
413	Mom:	Well I hope you were on your best behavior.
414	Sarah:	Oh, Mom, you know I was.
415	Mom:	I'm glad to hear that, sweetie.
416	Sarah:	Hey, Mom, I am hanging out with Lexy after soccer practice, right?
417	Mom:	Actually, soccer was cancelled because of the weather. I just checked my email before I left to pick you up.
418	Sarah:	Oh, that's too bad. I guess it is pretty cold and wet out here.

419	Mom:	Yeah, but you were supposed to go over to her house anyway.
420	Sarah:	Yes, I know. Where is Steven?
421	Mom:	He is resting in the car just over there.
422	Sarah:	Is he feeling any better?
423	Mom:	I think so. He is just tired and needs to rest. There is Lexy's mom.
424	Lexy:	Sarah! My mom is here to pick us up.
425	Sarah:	I know! I'm so excited.
426	Mom:	(To Lexy's mom) Are you sure you don't mind having Sarah over?
427	Susan:	It's not a problem. The girls have fun by themselves anyway. I hardly have to do anything.
428	Mom:	Oh, that's good.
429	Susan:	Besides, this way Steven can rest.
430	Mom:	Oh, yes, thank you. Sarah, have fun and be polite to Lexy's mother. I'll pick you up at five o'clock.
431	Sarah:	Okay. Bye Mom!
432	Susan:	Come on, girls. Let's get into the car before we get too cold and turn into icicles.
433	Sarah:	Your mom is so funny!
434	Lexy	(At Lexy's house) Do you want to play dress-up?
435	Sarah:	Yes! Can I wear the blue dress?
436	Lexy:	Sure. I'll wear the pink one and we can pretend that we are at the party waiting for the bad guys to come.
437	Sarah:	Then we can fight off the bad guys because we have to protect the prince.

438	Susan:	Would you girls like a snack? You know you can't fight bad guys on an empty stomach.
439	Lexy:	Oh, Mom, you're so goofy. Sure, we'll eat.
440	Susan:	I popped some popcorn and cut some peaches.
441	Sarah:	Thank you so much! I love peaches!
442	Susan:	You are more than welcome, Sarah. Thank you for having such good manners. Why don't you girls go wash your hands before you eat?
443	Sarah:	(The girls eat their snack.) Hey, Lexy, do you want to color?
444	Lexy:	I thought we were playing princesses.
445	Sarah:	Well, we are, but now we can be drawing princesses.
446	Lexy:	Okay! Do you want to use markers or crayons?
447	Sarah:	How about markers?
448	Lexy:	Okay. I'm going to draw a rainbow and lots of flowers.
449	Sarah:	That sounds nice. I'm going to draw lots and lots of butterflies.
450	Lexy:	We can use paint, too, if you want.
451	Sarah:	That's alright. I'm good with just markers.
452	Lexy:	Can you believe how Bryan acted at school today?
453	Sarah:	He was so stupid. I don't know why he keeps getting into trouble.
454	Lexy;	I think he was just trying to give the sub a hard time but it was just annoying.
455	Sarah:	I don't like him very much. He is not very nice.
456	Lexy:	Well, who do you like?

457	Sarah:	Don't tell anyone, but I have a secret crush on Connor.
458	Lexy:	Connor?
459	Sarah:	Yeah.
460	Lexy:	He is pretty cute, but I like Joe.
461	Sarah:	That's so funny!
462	Lexy:	Why do you say that?
463	Sarah:	Because they're best friends and we're best friends. That's why it's funny.
464	Lexy:	Oh, that is funny. Maybe we should write our silly story about that.
465	Sarah:	No way! We have to read those in front of the class and I don't want anyone to know.
466	Lexy:	Oh, that's right.
467	Susan:	Hey, girls, do you have any homework tonight?
468	Lexy:	No, Mom, we don't.
469	Susan:	Do you girls want to watch some TV?
470	Lexy:	What do you think, Sarah?
471	Sarah:	Sure, sounds good. What do you want to watch?
472	Lexy:	How about Jungle Junction©?
473	Sarah:	That sounds great. I love that show!
474	Lexy:	(The girls sit on the couch and watch the show.) Hey, let's pretend you are sleeping on the couch and only I can wake you up with my magic bracelet.
475	Kenny:	Can I play, too?
476	Lexy:	No little brothers allowed!
477	Kenny:	Oh, come on, I want to play.
478	Lexy	I said no! You always ruin our games.

479	Kenny:	I promise. I'll do whatever you say.
480	Lexy:	I don't think so.
481	Kenny:	Mom! Lexy won't let me play with her.
482	Susan:	Kenny, Lexy has a friend over right now, so why don't you let them play for a little while.
483	Kenny:	Hey, Lex, I'll even be a princess if you want.
484	Lexy:	Okay, fine, but you have to wear a dress and let me put bows in your hair.
485	Kenny:	No way, I'm not doing that.
486	Lexy:	Well, I guess you won't be playing with us then.
487	Sarah:	He can play. I don't mind.
488	Lexy:	Trust me. He's not like your little brother. He is not fun to play with.
489	Sarah:	Okay, back to the bracelet thing. I'm going to lie down.
490	Lexy:	Oh, no! It's Princess Sarah! Is she dead? I must put the magic bracelet on her wrist and save her.
491	Sarah:	(Slowly pretending to wake up) Princess Lexy! Thank you for rescuing me!
492	Lexy:	I thought you were dead!
493	Sarah:	No, just in a deep, magical sleep. The evil queen, Kenny, (the girls giggle) cast a spell on me. Thank goodness, you had the magic bracelet!
494	Lexy;	Come on, we must fight the evil queen together!
495	Lexy:	(The doorbell rings.) Oh, no! Is it five O'clock already?
496	Susan:	Sarah, your dad is here.

497	Sarah:	Daddy, I'm not ready. Can't I just stay a little while longer?
498	Dad:	No, Honey, we have to go home.
499	Lexy:	Mom, can Sarah stay for dinner?
500	Susan:	Not tonight, but maybe another time.
501	Dad:	Let's go, Sarah. Get your shoes on.
502	Sarah:	I don't know where they are.
503	Dad:	Well, you'd better hurry up and find them.
504	Susan:	I think you may have left them in the basement.
505	Sarah:	Oh, right. I'll go grab them.
506	Dad:	No playing around, Sarah. Just get your shoes and come right back up.
507	Sarah:	I will, Dad.
508	Dad:	Sarah, make sure you thank Lexy's mom for having you over today.
509	Sarah:	Thank you for having me over. It was a lot of fun.
510	Susan:	Anytime, sweetie.
511	Lexy:	Bye, Sarah, see you tomorrow.
512	Sarah:	Bye, Lex. Have fun with the evil queen (the girls start to giggle again)!
513	Susan:	I don't even know what they are talking about.
514	Dad:	(In the car) How was school today? Did you do anything fun?
515	Sarah:	We got to write a story about something silly that happened to us.
516	Dad:	What did you write about?
517	Sarah:	I wrote about the time when we were at the park and I thought I lost my shoe, but it was actually hiding on the slide.

518	Dad:	Did you? That was pretty funny.
519	Sarah:	It's a good thing we found the shoe, though. Those pink ones are my favorite.
520	Dad:	Yes, I remember that.
521	Sarah:	What are we going to do when we get home?
522	Dad:	We will have to make dinner, or at least help your mother.
523	Sarah:	Did you go to the store yet?
524	Dad:	I'm glad you asked. I completely forgot that I was supposed to go to the store!
525	Sarah:	Good thing I reminded you. You could have gotten in big trouble.
526	Dad:	You're right. Your mother would not have been very happy.
527	Dad:	(At the grocery store) Let's grab a cart.
528	Sarah:	Can I climb inside?
529	Dad:	No, there won't be any room left for the food.
530	Sarah:	Well, can I ride on the side of the cart then?
531	Dad:	That's fine, but hold on tight.
532	Sarah:	Can we buy some grapes?
533	Dad:	Grapes? Was that on the list?
534	Sarah:	I don't think so, but the red ones look so yummy!
535	Dad:	Sure, put some into the cart. They do look good. Maybe we should get some strawberries as well.
536	Sarah:	I'll grab them, Dad. And I definitely want pears, remember?
537	Dad:	Yes! What else do we need?
538	Sarah:	Dad, where is the list?

539	Dad:	I don't know. I think I may have left it at home.
540	Sarah:	We might be able to remember the things on the list between the two of us.
541	Dad:	I remember your mom asking for Jell-O for your brother.
542	Sarah:	And I think Mom said to get some bread, too.
543	Dad:	You have a great memory. I sure am glad to have you here with me!
544	Sarah:	I like going to the store with you, Daddy!
545	Dad:	So, what else do we need?
546	Sarah:	I know, I know! We need to get, Honey.
547	Dad:	Right! Now which aisle do we need to go to for, Honey? Oh, there it is, over on aisle six.
548	Sarah:	I think mom said something about crackers for Steven.
549	Dad:	You're right! With you here, who needs a list?
550	Sarah:	I guess I just have a good memory.
551	Dad:	No kidding! I think we're done. Let's go find a line to check-out.
552	Sarah:	Register fourteen just opened up.
553	Dad:	Quick, let's get over there before someone with eight hundred items lines up in front of us!
554	Checker:	Hi, there. Did you find everything you need alright?
555	Dad:	I think so.
556	Checker:	Good. That will be forty one twenty five ($41.25).
557	Checker:	(Dad hands him fifty dollars) Out of fifty? Eight seventy-five ($8.75) is your change.

558	Checker:	Do you need any help out to the car with your groceries?
559	Dad:	I think we got it, thanks.
560	Checker:	Thank you and have a great evening.
561	Dad:	You, too.
562	Sarah:	(after arriving home) Mom, we're home!
563	Mom:	Hey! Steven is still asleep.
564	Sarah:	Wow, he must be really sick.
565	Mom:	He's just really tired. His fever is gone and his temperature is normal so hopefully he will feel much better tomorrow. He got you a sticker from the doctor's office.
566	Sarah:	Wow, that was really nice of him! Hey, Mom, you should be really proud of me. Daddy and I went to the store but he forgot the list!
567	Dad:	Hey, you weren't supposed to tell on me!
568	Sarah:	Oops, sorry. Anyway, Daddy forgot the list and I remembered everything you told him to get!
569	Mom:	That's great, Sarah! I'm so proud of you. Now go wash-up, dinner is almost ready.
570	Sarah:	What are we having?
571	Mom:	Ginger chicken with brown rice and salad.
572	Sarah:	Mmmmm. I love your ginger chicken! Is Steven eating with us? Should I go wake him up?
573	Mom:	No, let him sleep. I don't think he will feel like eating right now.
574	Mom:	That's why I had you and Dad get some Jell-O and crackers.

575	Mom:	Maybe I'll make him some soup as well when he feels like eating.
576	Dad:	Do you need any help getting dinner ready?
577	Mom:	No, I think it is just about all done. If you could set the table, that would be great.
578	Sarah:	I can help you with that, too.
579	Mom:	(Sarah sets the table and the food is put on the table) Alright, let's sit down and eat.
580	Dad:	This looks great! Can you please pass the salad, Sarah?
581	Sarah:	Here you go.
582	Mom:	How was Lexy's today?
583	Sarah:	It was a lot of fun. Her little brother wanted to play with us, but we didn't let him.
584	Mom:	Well, that wasn't very nice. You let your brother play with you all the time.
585	Sarah:	Well, that's because he plays what we want to play and cooperates. Lexy's brother never listens.
586	Sarah:	We said he could be the evil queen and that was pretty funny.
587	Mom:	That is funny. Did he agree to it?
588	Sarah:	Well, sort of, but then Daddy came and we had to stop playing anyway.
589	Mom:	Ah, I see. Here, do you want some more rice?
590	Sarah:	Yes, please.
591	Sarah:	(they continue eating) May I please be excused?
592	Dad:	Did you get enough to eat?
593	Sarah:	I did.
594	Dad:	Sure. Please take your dishes to the sink.

595	Sarah:	Okay, Daddy.
596	Mom:	Why don't you go put away some of your art supplies?
597	Sarah:	I'll do that. When I'm done with that, can you read me a book?
598	Mom:	Well, after we get cleaned up here, and you take your bath and when you're in bed, I suppose.
599	Sarah:	That sounds good. Can I take a bubble bath?
600	Mom:	Sure.
601	Dad:	Why don't you start her bath? I will finish the dishes.
602	Mom	That works for me. Come on, sweetie, let's get those dirty clothes off.
603	Sarah:	I'll start putting the bubbles in when you start the water.
604	Mom:	How does the water feel?
605	Sarah:	Too cold! Make it warmer!
606	Mom:	How about now?
607	Sarah:	Much better. Can I wash my own hair? I'm eight (8) now and I can do it all by myself.
608	Mom:	Sure, but I'm going to help you rinse it since you have such thick hair and it's hard to get all the shampoo out sometimes.
609	Sarah:	Okay. Have you seen my favorite ducky toy?
610	Mom:	I'll go check in the shower. I think you may have left it in there last time.
611	Sarah:	Thanks, Mom. I'm all done with the shampoo. Can you rinse it out now?
612	Mom:	Okay, lean your head back so I don't get water or soap in your eyes.

613	Sarah:	Can I put conditioner in, too?
614	Mom:	Yes, then wash your body.
615	Sarah:	I don't know how I got paint on my elbow today, but somehow I did.
616	Mom:	Scrub it well.
617	Sarah:	Okay, I think I'm all done in here.
618	Mom:	Do a final rinse and grab your towel. Which pajamas do you want to wear?
619	Sarah:	Is it going to be cold tonight?
620	Mom:	Probably.
621	Sarah:	I'll wear the fuzzy snowman one.
622	Mom:	Alright, brush your teeth while I get those for you.
623	Sarah:	Okay.
624	Mom:	Good girl.
625	Dad:	Are you almost ready for bed?
626	Sarah:	Almost. Will you read me books tonight?
627	Dad:	I would love to. We can read three. Which ones do you want to read?
628	Sarah:	Let me think. How about "The Bear Snores On", "The Three Bad Pigs", and "The Happy Dolphin"?
629	Dad:	Those sound great. Why don't you go find them and I'll be in your room in five minutes?
630	Sarah:	Okay, Daddy.
631	Mom:	Goodnight, sweetie. Sweet dreams!
632	Sarah:	Goodnight, Mom.
633	Dad:	Let's snuggle up and read!
634	Sarah:	(They read the three books) Daddy, I need to go to the bathroom.
635	Dad:	Go on then.

636	Note:	(Sarah goes and then crawls back into bed)
637	Sarah:	Daddy, can you get me some water?
638	Dad:	Sure, Honey.
639	Sarah:	Daddy, I'm hungry.
640	Dad:	I'm sorry, but you've already brushed your teeth. Next time, eat more at dinner or have a snack before brushing your teeth.
641	Sarah:	Alright.
642	Dad:	Goodnight, sleep tight, don't let the bedbugs bite!
643	Sarah:	Wait, don't turn all the lights off.
644	Dad:	Alright, I'll just dim it. How is this?
645	Sarah:	Great. Can I listen to my lullaby CD?
646	Dad:	Sure. Anything else?
647	Sarah:	Nope. 'Night, Dad. I love you.
648	Dad:	I love you, too.
649	Sarah:	(A few minutes go by) Daddy! I'm lonely. Can I sleep with Steven?
650	Dad:	Not tonight. He needs a good night's sleep. Besides, I think he's snoring. Here's an extra stuffed animal to cuddle with.
651	Sarah:	Thanks.
652	Dad:	(10 minutes go by and the dad peeks in on Sarah) Sarah, what are you still doing up?
653	Sarah:	I wasn't tired so I thought I would read some more books.
654	Dad:	Only for a few minutes, then you really need to go to sleep.
655	Sarah:	Okay. (Dad comes in a few minutes later and she is asleep)